CATASTROPHES
& HEROES

Also by Jerry Borrowman

Beyond the Call of Duty

Compassionate Soldier

Invisible Heroes of World War II

TRUE STORIES OF MAN-MADE DISASTERS

CATASTROPHES & HEROES

JERRY BORROWMAN

SHADOW
MOUNTAIN

Visit us at shadowmountain.com

Library of Congress Cataloging-in-Publication Data
(CIP data on file)
ISBN 978-1-62972-739-4

Printed in the United States of America
Lake Book Manufacturing, Inc., Melrose Park, IL

10 9 8 7 6 5 4 3 2 1

*This book is dedicated to all the first-responder heroes
who rush toward a disaster to offer help while others are fleeing.
Thank you for your courage, bravery, and willingness to
risk your health and lives in moments of crisis.*

CONTENTS

ACKNOWLEDGMENTS

I'd like to express appreciation to my wife, Marcella Borrowman, for her insightful story edit and to my readers' panel for the time they spent reviewing the text, correcting errors, and improving the storytelling. Thank you to Brian Ellis, Norman Jenson, Bill Gallagher, Sharron and Tom Sandquist, J. R. Jones, Kelissa Peterson, and Dennis Russell.

INTRODUCTION

We live in a world in which we are completely dependent on an almost invisible but highly engineered infrastructure that makes modern life possible. Technology enables us to flip a light switch that is always connected to a reliable source of electricity, turn a tap that brings fresh water, and drive on roads that effortlessly span chasms and bodies of water without a pause. But behind all these conveniences are massive dams and bridges funded by taxpayers. Privately maintained railroad tracks enable high-speed trains to move millions of railcars filled with food and other vital commodities. Power companies use a variety of fuels to create and distribute electricity. And all this is so well-designed that we hardly give it a thought, at least until something goes wrong. Then something does go wrong—severe weather, sabotage, poor design or workmanship, lack of maintenance—and a catastrophe strikes.

Following are eight stories of spectacular failures that caused great suffering and loss of life. Each story has five parts: (1) an overview of the disaster; (2) the fateful choices that led to the disaster; (3) the unintended consequences; (4) the heroic efforts involved in the disaster, including the first-responder heroes who risked their lives to save others, and then the professional, regulatory, or governmental heroes who fought for permanent change to avoid future catastrophes; then (5) the lessons learned by those responsible for either the disaster or its cleanup.

In each situation, a person in authority had a decision to make—to follow best practices or to take shortcuts. These disasters were preventable, but those who should have acted better failed to do so because of incompetence, greed, or malice.

After the failures, it fell to others to help rescue those who were injured and to then help the affected communities rebuild. Heroic efforts were made to save the victims and offer relief to the suffering. The rescuers' stories are inspiring.

Finally, lessons were learned from each tragedy and steps were taken to prevent the mistakes from happening again. An important and redemptive part of each story is that from tragedy comes progress.

The stories are told in chronological order, starting in 1865 with the Mississippi steamboat *Sultana* and ending in 1963 with Italy's Vajont Dam. I hope you enjoy learning about these stories as much as I have.

CHAPTER 1

1865: PRISONERS ON THE MISSISSIPPI

THE HUMAN COST OF TRAGEDY

"My experience on that terrible morning no pen can write, nor tongue can tell. I was thrown into the surging waves of that mighty river, into the jaws of death. Life depended on one grand effort, expert swimming, which I did successfully, and after swimming six or seven miles, according to statements given by citizens living on the banks of the river, landed on the Arkansas shore without any assistance whatever. There I found a confederate soldier who came to my relief, and took me to a house nearby, and gave me something to eat, and I felt something like myself again, thanks to the Great Ruler of the Universe. The said confederate soldier worked hard to save the lives of the drowning men and brought to shore in his little dugout about fifteen of them."

—P. S. Atchley, a Union soldier from Trotter's Store, Tennessee[1]

OVERVIEW

Perhaps the greatest of all the suffering in the Civil War was that endured by the Union soldiers held as prisoners of war in Andersonville, Georgia. In Andersonville, some 32,000 men were crammed into a camp designed to support 10,000. Sanitation was appalling, with one small creek acting as both sewer and the source of drinking water. Dysentery and malaria were rampant. The soldiers were supposed to receive the same food ration as active-duty Confederate soldiers, but Georgia's food supply was largely destroyed, so the prisoners received only meager rations. This included a daily portion of rancid grain or a cupful of cornmeal and perhaps a teaspoon or two of boiled peas or beans flavored with a few ounces of raw bacon or beef. This diet led to scurvy, malnutrition, and starvation. With no medical service to help them, 12,912 prisoners died while in captivity, an appalling 30 percent of those incarcerated. This photo of an Andersonville survivor shows the desperate condition in which the men struggled to stay alive.

The liberation of the camp at the end of the Civil War was an event that should have brought joy to the prisoners, but most were too weak to celebrate. Still, the promise of returning to their homes in the North offered hope. As soon as they were healthy enough to travel, a group of 2,000 liberated prisoners were transferred to Camp Fisk, near the Mississippi town of Vicksburg. Their official status was "paroled" until they went north to be mustered out of the Union army. Until then, they remained under guard and subject to the orders of their superior officers. It was at Vicksburg that they would transfer to steamboats headed

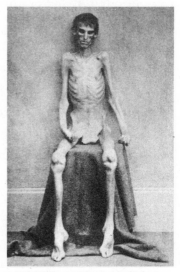

A liberated prisoner of war from Andersonville.

upstream on the Mississippi River. Then they would travel on to their homes in Ohio, Michigan, Indiana, Kentucky, and Virginia.

But unknown to these paroled prisoners, even after all that they had endured, a new danger awaited them, a danger that was preventable except for the greed and avarice of two corrupt individuals.

THE STEAMSHIP *SULTANA*

In 1810, there were just twenty steamboats on the Mississippi River and its tributaries. By 1830, there were more than 1,200, and the number continued to grow until the outbreak of the Civil War. Through an intricate web of rivers and canals, it was possible to ship goods by river faster and at far less expense than by land-based transportation.

The inland steamboats of the era were engineering marvels. They opened nearly two million square miles of land to settlement and trade that today would include rivers in thirty-two states. The secret to their success was in the design of their flat-bottomed hulls, which drew just five to seven feet of water while supporting thousands of tons of superstructure, cargo, and passengers. A typical mid-century steamboat could easily transport 250 passengers *and* 10,000 bales of cotton, large quantities of livestock, and other cargo.

The steamship Sultana *at Memphis, April 26, 1865.*

In water that was often not as deep as a person is tall, these powerful steamboats made their way upstream against the current from New Orleans to Pittsburgh. A common joke of the time was that a Mississippi steamboat could "navigate on heavy dew." It was an awesome sight to see hundreds of steamboats lined up at the wharfs of New Orleans and St. Louis as river traffic exploded, bringing new prosperity to the interior of the United States.

In January 1863, the new four-deck steamboat *Sultana* was launched into the Ohio River at Cincinnati, weighing 1,719 tons. It was nearly the length of a football field at 260 feet, but the beam was just forty-two feet wide, giving the boat a long and sleek profile. The *Sultana* was powered by four high-pressure fire-tube boilers that fed steam to the two piston engines that turned the massive thirty-four-foot waterwheels on each side of the boat at midships. Each engine consisted of a horizontal cylinder that measured twenty-five inches in diameter with an eight-foot stroke of the piston. At almost 2,500 horsepower, the power plant was strong enough to propel the steamboat more than ten miles per hour upstream against a current of five to six miles per hour.

With an elegantly furnished main cabin on the second deck and thirty-four private staterooms, the *Sultana* furnished unrivaled comfort to the highest-paying passengers. White-gloved waiters set up tables in the main cabin for each of the meals while entertainment played from the stage. Deck passengers didn't have nearly the same level of comfort, but their fare was substantially less and still included good food and a quick travel time.

Having been commissioned during the Civil War, the *Sultana* spent most of her first two years carrying troops downriver to support the Union military campaigns against the Confederacy. Now, in April 1865, she was about to bring some of those troops back north, including those who had been imprisoned at the Andersonville and Cahaba prison camps.

FATEFUL CHOICES

JAMES MASON AND REUBEN HATCH

Captain James C. Mason was the second riverboat captain to command the *Sultana*. He and two other St. Louis investors had purchased the boat from Captain Preston Lodwick in the spring of 1864. It was not unusual for a captain to also be an owner, although it created a potential conflict of interest between safe operation and the profitability of the ship. Such was the case in the early months of 1865, when river traffic fell precipitously because of the collapse of the Confederacy. Revenue was so low that Mason had to sell off two shares of his interest in the *Sultana* to maintain operating capital. He saw the opportunity to make a quick profit by transporting the liberated prisoners of Camp Fisk upriver as vital to his financial viability. It is also likely why he agreed to pay a kickback to Colonel Reuben Hatch of the Union army, the chief quartermaster in Vicksburg, Mississippi. Quartermaster Hatch was responsible for selecting the steamboats that would transfer the prisoners north at a price of $2.75 per enlisted man and $8.00 per officer. In exchange for a bribe, Hatch offered to fill Mason's boat with paroled prisoners, and Mason agreed. The deal was struck at a meeting in Hatch's office in Vicksburg on April 17, 1865.

Here's how things unfolded. The *Sultana* had been in Cairo, Illinois, on April 15 when news arrived that President Abraham Lincoln had been assassinated. Mason realized that because most of the telegraph lines to the Mississippi River towns downriver were inoperable, he had a chance to bring this awful but essential news to those cities. This humanitarian reporting would enhance his reputation on the river and hopefully bring new business. Grabbing a stack of black-rimmed newspapers, he shrouded the *Sultana* in black bunting and steamed downriver. In each town, the people reacted with shock and sadness to his news. On the morning of April 17, the

Sultana pulled into the wharf at Vicksburg to deliver the grim news. That's when Hatch and Mason agreed to the compensation scheme.

Colonel Reuben Hatch had a checkered past, and many believed he should have been sent to prison. For example, in 1861, Reuben Hatch had been appointed as the assistant quartermaster in Cairo at the urging of his brother. In this post, which is responsible for securing and distributing supplies to the military, Hatch and a friend had entered into below-market-cost lumber contracts with local dealers and then sold the lumber to the federal government at market prices. The difference in price was an illegal rebate that enriched Hatch and his partner. This went on until the lumber dealers realized what was happening and went to the *Chicago Tribune* to report the cheating. The ensuing scandal was an embarrassment to Hatch's commanding officer, General Ulysses S. Grant, who ordered an immediate investigation. It turned out that lumber wasn't the only scam that Hatch was running. He'd inflated the price of government-issued clothing and had chartered steamboats at one price while charging the government a higher price, embezzling the difference. When Hatch became aware of the investigation, he threw his incriminating ledgers into the Ohio River. Unfortunately for him, they washed up on shore a few days later, providing irrefutable proof of his crimes.

General Grant ordered a military tribunal, but Reuben Hatch's brother Ozias, the secretary of state for Illinois, sent a written appeal to President Lincoln, asking him to intervene. He told Lincoln that the investigation was "without merit" and should be dropped. Because Ozias had been a prominent fundraiser for Lincoln's presidential campaign, his letter carried real weight. Even more so since it was cosigned by Illinois governor Richard Bates and state auditor Jesse Dubois. In response, Lincoln wrote a letter to the judge advocate vouching for Reuben Hatch's integrity and suggesting that the charges be investigated by a civilian tribunal appointed by Illinois politicians rather than a military tribunal. Despite 1,600 separate and well-documented incidents of fraud, this political panel exonerated Reuben Hatch. He escaped prosecution, but his reputation in the military was ruined, and he resigned.

Two years later, with new help from his brother, he requested reappointment to the army in March 1865. Just two months earlier, an examining board responsible for rating potential quartermasters had reported that "of the 60 officers who have appeared before this board, not more than 1 or 2 can compare with Colonel Hatch in degree of *deficiency.* . . . He is totally unfit to discharge the duties of assistant quartermaster."[2]

The board had essentially blacklisted Hatch from further service. Yet, with a new recommendation from Lincoln to Secretary of War Edwin Stanton, Hatch was appointed chief quartermaster in Vicksburg, Mississippi. The fox was placed in charge of the henhouse, with thousands of government dollars at his disposal.

Two Ships Empty, the *Sultana* Overcrowded

The *Sultana* completed its journey to New Orleans and made a quick turnaround so Captain Mason could make it back to Vicksburg to pick up the Union soldiers paroled by the Confederacy. But ten hours south of Vicksburg, the chief engineer reported that one of the four boilers had developed a leak in a seam and a bulge in an iron plate. It forced him to take that boiler offline, which slowed the upstream speed of the ship. This frustrated Captain Mason, but he needn't have worried. While he was away, Colonel Hatch had sent two empty steamboats upriver, even as several thousand troops waited restlessly for their transport north.

Knowing that his timing was precarious, Mason tracked down a boiler repairman as soon as the *Sultana* docked in Vicksburg and browbeat him into working through the night to repair the leaky boiler. The boilermaker thought the damage to the boiler was severe enough to warrant a major repair job to replace several sheets of riveted iron and hammer out the bulge. But Captain Mason insisted on a temporary repair that would get the boat north to Cincinnati, where the more extensive repair work could be done. The boiler-maker reluctantly agreed and set to work placing a patch on the fractured seam. He warned the chief engineer, Nathan Wintringer, to monitor the water level carefully, since the boiler was likely to experience a potentially fatal hotspot at the site of the repair.

When Mason first arrived in Vicksburg, it looked like only five hundred troops would be ready to transfer north. He threw a fit, demanding that he get at least the thousand soldiers promised to him. "Otherwise," he stated, "it would be better to leave port immediately with no soldiers." This would have meant no bribe money for Hatch, and it moved him to action. By early the next day, nearly two thousand soldiers started boarding the *Sultana* even as a third steamboat lay empty and willing to take on a share of the prisoners.

Given that the *Sultana* was designed for just 360 passengers, two thousand was overloading on an unprecedented scale.

By debarkation time, the *Sultana* was weighed down by an estimated 1,961 paroled Union soldiers, twenty-two guards, seventy paying cabin passengers, and eighty-five crew members, for a total of 2,138 people! So heavy was this mass of people on the upper decks that the crew members frantically installed additional timber support stanchions between the lower and upper decks to support the weight. The men complained that there was little room to lie down and sleep, let alone respond to the call of nature using only two small latrines.

Despite the complaints, the *Sultana* pulled away from the Vicksburg wharf with this mass of humanity on the evening of April 25, 1865. Although the voyage promised him a handsome payout of nearly $6,000 for a single trip north, minus the bribe, even Captain Mason was worried about the overcrowding, since he was now in charge of the safety of all these people.

The biggest problem from an operational point of view was that the *Sultana* was top-heavy. The people crowded on the upper decks raised the center of gravity, putting the steamboat way out of balance. This made it prone to careening from side to side. So severe was this problem that when the boat docked in Memphis, Tennessee, and a photographer asked the men to come to the shore side for a photo, Mason had to scream at them to get back to the other side to bring the boat back into trim (balance).

Mason knew it was urgent. Besides making the boat difficult to maneuver, not being on an even keel would aggravate the risk of a boiler explosion. Boiler explosions had destroyed more than 230 inland steamboats in the previous fifty years, so Mason was wise to worry about this risk—particularly since he was relying on a boiler already weakened from the earlier leak.

UNINTENDED CONSEQUENCES

APRIL 27, 1865—FIRE IN THE NIGHT SKY!

With the boilers operating at full capacity, the steamboat churned its way upstream, with stops in Greenville, Mississippi; Helena, Arkansas; and Memphis, Tennessee. There they took on fresh water and additional food. At 1:00 A.M. on the morning of April 27, the *Sultana* chugged out of Memphis to rendezvous with a coal barge on the opposite side of the river, where they loaded an additional 75,000 pounds of coal.

At approximately 2:00 A.M., seven miles north of Memphis, an unprecedented disaster struck. Here is how Sally M. Walker describes it in her book *Sinking the* Sultana:

"Suddenly, with a loud roar, one of the *Sultana*'s boilers burst. Within seconds, two more boilers exploded. Steam and chunks of red-hot iron blasted upward through the center of the boat. The explosive force shattered the support structures of the main and cabin decks as if they were toothpicks. Within a minute, both decks had collapsed behind the main stairway in the center of the boat. A gaping hole replaced the staterooms and cabin area located above the boilers. Surrounding the hole, the cabin deck's broken floorboards slanted toward the fireboxes left exposed after the boilers exploded.

A contemporary illustration of the Sultana *on fire.*

The *Sultana's* two chimneys, robbed of their support, toppled and crashed onto the hurricane deck. Hundreds of men on the collapsed cabin and smashed hurricane decks slid toward and then dropped into the fireboxes' blazing coals.

"Steam blasted through the hurricane deck as rapidly as it had ripped through the lower decks and hurtled splintered boards through the air like spears. Three-fourths of the texas deck was obliterated. The force of the blast flung First Mate Rowberry out of the pilothouse and into the cold river, about forty feet from the boat. When he surfaced, the river 'was full, a sea of heads for hundreds of yards around.' Screams for help came from all directions. Mangled bodies floated in the water. Damage to the pilothouse and steering wheel left the *Sultana* at the mercy of the Mississippi."[3]

The nightmare of an explosion had come true; hundreds of people, including the prisoners from Andersonville, were either killed directly or were at risk of drowning in the icy waters of the Mississippi. Hundreds more were burned or scalded, others impaled by exploding debris, and still others who were awakened from sleep were too dazed to understand what was happening. Many were terrified of plunging into the river, since they didn't know how to swim. Yet the *Sultana* was on fire, flames spreading fore and aft from midship, even as the boat started drifting helplessly with the current. Those who leapt over the starboard side were at risk of having the steamer crush them as it swung out into the current. Some of the surviving deckhands managed to swing a lifeboat out into the river. Dozens of people leaping from the *Sultana* capsized the lifeboat, sending it downstream empty. Others grabbed whatever they could that would float and hurled themselves into the river to escape the flames. Wooden deck chairs, furniture, and shattered pieces of the boat itself became their only hope of survival as they gasped for air in the cold, muddy waters of the river.

Some of the passengers later related that they had seen Captain Mason breaking up pieces of wood and other floatable remains of the boat to hand to passengers. They said he stayed on the *Sultana* so long trying to save others that he eventually drowned.

VICTIMS AND FIRST-RESPONDER HEROES

A Survivor's Account

With hundreds of passengers who were not killed by the explosion, there are many stories of what it was like to be on the burning ship and to then jump into the freezing waters of the Mississippi River, far from either shore. This account from Hosea C. Aldrich must stand as representative of the many:

"I enlisted in the service of the United States in August, 1862, in Hillsdale county, Mich., as sergeant in Company G of the 18th Mich. Vol. Inft. I was captured at Athens, Ala., on the 24th of September, 1864, and was confined in prison at Cahaba, Ala., and released from there April 12, 1865, and sent to Vicksburg, Miss., where I went on board the boiler deck of the steamer 'Sultana' with the other prisoners, like a flock of sheep, until her passengers numbered 2,141—over six times her capacity . . .

"We left Memphis about one o'clock A.M. April 27th. There was no danger manifested, and more than that it was not in the least anticipated only that the boat was heavily loaded. But in the darkness of that morning, between one and two o'clock opposite [Tagleman] Landing, eight miles above Memphis, suddenly and without warning, the boiler of the steamer exploded. When it happened I was sound asleep, and the first thing that I knew or heard was a terrible crash, everything seemed to be falling. The things I had under my head, my shoes, and some other articles and specimens that I had gathered up and had tied up in an old pair of drawers, they all went down through the floor. We scrambled back. The smoke came rushing up through the passage made by the exit of the exploded boiler. The cry from all was, 'What is the matter?' and the reply came, 'The boat is on fire.' It was all confusion. The screams of women and children mingled with the groans of the wounded and dying. Brave men rushed to and fro in the agony of fear, some uttering the most profane language and others commending their spirits to the Great Ruler of the Universe; the cries of the drowning and the roaring of the flames as they leaped heavenward made the scene most affecting and touching. But it was of short duration as the glare that illuminated the sky and made visible the awful despair of the hour soon died away while darkness more intense than ever settled down on the floating hulk and the victims of the disaster. I was pushed in the water and started for the bottom of the Mississippi, but I soon rose to the surface and found a small piece of board, and soon had the luck of getting a larger board, which was very lucky for me, as I could not swim. . . . We floated along down the river nearly an hour I think when my limbs began to cramp; that was the last of which I was conscious until at eight o'clock A.M. We had floated down the river six miles and lodged in the flood-wood against an island which was within two miles of Memphis, and here were picked up by the United States picket boat, 'Pocahontas.' They poured whiskey down me, rolled and rubbed me, and finally brought me back to life. I was like the new born babe, not a raveling of clothing upon me, in a place surrounded by persons whom I had never seen before, but I was happy as a lark to think I was rescued and saved. They placed me on a stretcher and carried me to the Overton hospital at Memphis, gave me a shirt and drawers and placed me in a good bunk. The third day, as soon as I was able to get up, they issued a suit of Uncle Sam's blues for me and I was happy, without as much as a postage stamp, for I thought I might live so as to tell the story to friends at home, and I am glad that I have the opportunity to give this short and hasty sketch. I was discharged from the service of the United States at Jackson, Mich., July 1865."[4]

Shortly after the explosion, those onboard the steamboat *Bostona II* saw a glow coming from the direction of Memphis as they sailed south from Cairo, Illinois, upstream of the *Sultana*. Rounding a bend, they saw the *Sultana* burning and witnessed the smokestacks collapsing to the deck. Hearing the cries of hundreds of people in the water, they immediately launched their yawl and began to pluck survivors out of the river. Captain Watson of the *Bostona II* ordered his men to throw anything over the side of the steamer that could assist people in the water, including gangplanks, tables, chairs, and more. Their yawl made nine trips out and back, saving more than two hundred people from freezing to death in the icy waters of the river.

Eventually, Captain Watson realized that there were simply too many people in the river for his crew to save. He made the difficult decision to bring his engines to full speed and race to Memphis to alert others so they could assist in the rescue operation. As the alarm spread, other steamboats paddled out into the river and headed upstream to help. Military gunboats still in service to the Union navy were especially effective. Their crews launched their small boats into the river, pulling hundreds from the water. They were often guided only by the cries of pain and suffering. During the night of the explosion, the survivors were tormented by both their burns and the icy water. When morning arrived, millions of hungry mosquitoes added to their torment.

By midday on April 27, the river was mostly quiet. Many who

had survived the initial explosion later drowned after succumbing to exhaustion or hypothermia. Still, the boats in the area continued to search the islands and marshes along the banks of the river, where some survivors had managed to pull themselves from the water, hoping for rescue. Throughout the day, these survivors were delivered to area hospitals, where they were received by medical teams who were well-prepared from their experience in the Civil War.

Of the estimated 2,138 people on board the *Sultana* at the time of the explosion, it is believed that 1,169 died, leaving 969 survivors. The numbers are uncertain because the record of those who boarded was made in haste, and many survivors made their way out of Memphis before they were accounted for. Each of the survivors had a harrowing tale to tell. Many had debilitating injuries that plagued them for the rest of their lives. The explosion of the *Sultana* was the deadliest maritime disaster in US history until the Japanese attack on Pearl Harbor in 1941.

PUBLIC REACTION

Given that the loss of life and the injuries sustained from the *Sultana* constituted the greatest maritime disaster in United States history to that point in time, it is surprising that almost no one knows about it today. Even in 1865, it received little national attention. The main reason for this was that it occurred just twelve days after President Abraham Lincoln died from the wounds he had received at Ford's Theater, and the attention of the country was riveted on his death and funeral.

People recognized that it was Lincoln's tenacity, drive, and inspiring leadership that had finally resolved the issues that had divided the country since its founding. Because of Lincoln, the Union had been saved; the Emancipation Proclamation had freed the slaves in all states then in rebellion; and the Thirteenth Amendment to the US Constitution was passed to forever prohibit slavery and indentured servitude. Lincoln's initial goal had been to prevent secession, but his legacy was the ending of slavery and the reuniting of the country. His death was deeply felt, and his assassination preoccupied the country. As a result, the *Sultana* story was relegated to the back pages of the newspapers.

A second reason that the *Sultana* story was not widely covered was that it occurred within just a few weeks of the ending of the Civil War, a war which had caused 650,000 deaths and wounded 470,000. The death of an additional 1,169 on the Mississippi was tragic, but it was a tragedy swallowed up in an ocean of suffering.

REPARATIONS

Of the 969 survivors, most had already suffered great deprivation while imprisoned at Andersonville Prison, only to be subjected to the ordeal of the *Sultana* explosion. Many suffered scalding burns, had their lungs damaged from blasts of steam, or received other serious injuries. Yet no additional compensation, beyond the small pension that was given to all veterans, was ever awarded to these men. Several bills were introduced into Congress to provide financial relief, but all failed. The steamboat company was bankrupted by the incident, and Hatch and others involved had safely insulated themselves from financial responsibility. The survivors were left on their own to survive in the postwar world—even those whose disabilities severely limited or excluded their active participation in the workforce.

PROFESSIONAL HEROES—ACTING TO PREVENT FUTURE TRAGEDY

CAUSES OF THE DISASTER INVESTIGATED

General Cadwallader Washburn made his way to Memphis by noon of the day of the disaster to investigate the cause of the explosion, even as survivors were still being pulled from the river. Second engineer Samuel Clemens,[5] who was severely injured and just moments away from dying, said that while he had thought the repairs completed in Vicksburg were adequate when they left port, he now believed that the repair was defective and was the cause of the first explosion. But Clemens also reported that the boat had careened considerably just moments before the explosion, because it was top-heavy. He died shortly after providing this testimony.

There were many who believed that the explosion was an act of sabotage by Confederate sympathizers who were intent on killing Union soldiers. Some suggested that a coal torpedo had been mixed in with the coal. These fist-sized metal nuggets, disguised as pieces of coal and filled with several ounces of gunpowder, had been used earlier in the war. But a team of investigators at the wreck site examined the pattern of the explosion and concluded that it was caused by weakened metal, rather than by an explosive device. For one thing, a gunpowder explosion would have blasted down through the deck. The steam explosion had shot upward at a forty-five-degree angle towards the back of the boat, leaving the hull largely undamaged but the superstructure in shambles. Still, people speculated it was sabotage for decades after the explosion, with some even bragging that they had caused it. The army dismissed these claims as false. Once sabotage was eliminated as a potential cause, the investigations concluded that hotspots in the weakened boiler metal were responsible.

Here's how it works. In a high-pressure steam boiler, it is essential that all boiler surfaces be continually bathed in water to prevent the metal from overheating. But it's also critical that enough headroom be left for the steam to accumulate. Thus it's a constant balancing act of adding new water to the boiler as steam is distributed to the engines. Too much water, and the engines become sluggish from lack of steam. Too little water, and the exposed tubes or base plate become dangerously hot, which leads to a flash of steam that reverberates within the boiler at high velocity, initiating a cascade of failure. If the boat tilts downward to either the starboard or port side, the water in the boiler sloshes to that side. If the water level is

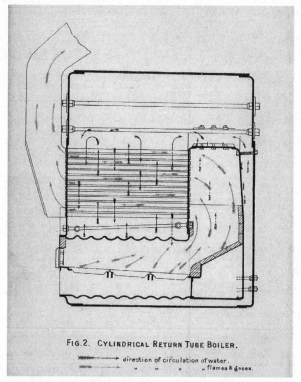

FIG.2. CYLINDRICAL RETURN TUBE BOILER.

━━━▶ direction of circulation of water.
━━━ „ „ „ „ flames & gases.

A schematic of a cylindrical water boiler similar to the Sultana*'s.*

too low, some of the fire tubes on the rising side of the boiler are left exposed without the protective water bath, and the temperature of the metal soars. When the water sloshes back over this now searing-hot metal, it flashes into steam with an instantaneous expansion ratio of 1:1,700. Because the exposed metal is white-hot, the conversion to steam is instantaneous.

This blast of superheated steam displaces the water around it in an explosive fashion, sending a shock wave through the rest of the boiler, smashing into the metal on the opposite side. If the metal on that side is fatigued or weakened from sedimentation hotspots or a faulty repair (as in the *Sultana*), it ruptures from the force, allowing steam to escape the boiler. This rapid escape of steam from the ruptured spot quickly leads to a catastrophic failure, because as the boiler pressure drops from releasing steam, the boiling point of water also decreases, vaporizing *all the remaining water* in the boiler in a single, massive flash. It is this secondary explosion that blows the boiler to pieces.

A secondary explosion was what destroyed the *Sultana* on April 27, 1865. Shrapnel from the first boiler explosion punctured the adjacent boilers, which led to similar expansive explosions in them.

What is not known is whether the precipitating boiler explosion was caused by the rolling of the ship because the boat was top-heavy, or if the explosion was simply a failure of the Vicksburg repair to withstand so much steam while trying to move the heavily laden ship upstream against a flooding current.

The answer would properly assign responsibility for the failure. If it was due to excessive careening, then the blame for the disaster fell squarely on the shoulders of those who overcrowded the upper decks of the ship. Captain Mason and Colonel Hatch were the two men most responsible for putting more than 2,000 people on a boat designed for 365.

If, on the other hand, the blast was the result of a failed patch to the boiler, then the explosion would have happened regardless of the number of people on board. But even if this *was* the cause, the loss of life and injury was amplified because of the extensive overcrowding.

In either event, the blame points to Hatch, the quartermaster who never would have been in the position to overload the ship had it not been for the intervention of Abraham Lincoln at the time of his appointment and promotion.

Yet Hatch was never convicted for his role in the disaster, because he shrewdly resigned his commission before the court was convened. The military no longer had jurisdiction over Hatch, and no civilian court asserted authority to try what was viewed as a military matter. It was a brilliant move on Hatch's part, particularly since he immediately left Vicksburg and headed north, where he was out of reach of those conducting the inquiries. Not that they didn't try to hear from him; he simply refused to comply with three summonses to appear and offer testimony. By doing so, he evaded any legal responsibility for his actions.

In the end, no one was held responsible for the sinking, except perhaps for Captain James Cass Mason, who lost his life along with so many passengers as a result of the explosion.

SAFETY IMPROVEMENTS MADE BECAUSE OF THE *SULTANA* DISASTER

While the *Sultana* explosion did not garner the national attention it deserved, the awful impact of the tragedy was felt by those who operated steamboats on the river. Meaningful changes were implemented as a result of professional investigations into the *Sultana* explosion, which saved many other lives from similar explosions, including:

- The type of iron used in the *Sultana* boilers was discontinued on all new steamboats. It had proved itself increasingly brittle under repeated heating and cooling cycles, which made it susceptible to rupture.

- Steamboats reverted to using a two-tube boiler design, in which two large gas tubes passed through the water bath, rather than the twenty-four smaller firetubes in the *Sultana*'s "tubular boiler." The two-tube design was less efficient but was easier to maintain and less inclined to accrue sedimentation and the accompanying hot spots that would weaken the boiler metal.

- Finally, with the end of the war, normal civilian safety rules regulating the maximum number of passengers and freight tonnage were reimplemented and tightened. Military officers like Reuben Hatch could no longer use their wartime authority to override safety protocols.

These changes improved safety for passengers and crews alike, giving some meaning to the additional suffering and deaths of the prisoners who faced their final trial of the war on the steamboat *Sultana* on April 27, 1865.

CHAPTER 2

1879: SCOTLAND'S TAY RAILWAY BRIDGE

THE HUMAN COST OF TRAGEDY

Janet Mitchell stirred as her husband, David, quietly slipped out of bed at 5:00 A.M. on a bleak Sunday morning in late December 1879. It was cold outside, and she would soon have to get up to fix breakfast for their four young children. At least David would add new fuel to the fire to warm the kitchen, making her job just a little easier. She heard him fixing himself breakfast and then he slipped in to give her a kiss on the cheek before he stepped out into the winter darkness. It was not unusual for David, a railroad engineer, to rise early to prepare the Edinburgh Express for its journey south from Dundee to the north shore of the Firth of Forth just north of Edinburgh, Scotland, but it was unusual for a Sunday morning.

Janet appreciated the income that David's skilled work provided, but always felt uneasy because of the danger involved in the high-speed work that took David from her. No one knows what she and her husband said to each other that morning, but it's unlikely she had any thought that this day would be unlike any other in their lives, or that her world was about to change forever.

OVERVIEW

THE BEAUTIFUL RAILWAY BRIDGE ACROSS THE FIRTH OF TAY

On the night of December 28, 1879, gale-force winds blew from the west down the Tay River estuary at Dundee, where the river empties into the North Sea. With sustained winds of approximately fifty miles per hour and gusts of up to eighty miles per hour, the wind tore slate shingles from rooftops, sent tavern signs flying through the streets, and blew three railcars loaded with ten tons of coal nearly four hundred yards *uphill* before attendants could block the wheels.

Most of the residents of Dundee sheltered in their homes. Some watched the estuary from upstairs windows. There, the pride of the British North Railway stood staunchly against the storm—the nineteen-month-old Tay Bridge. They knew that the last train of that wintry Sunday was scheduled at 7:10 P.M.

The Tay Bridge was an engineering marvel. It was the longest bridge in the world at the time, spanning two miles of water at a height of up to eighty-eight feet above the crest of the river. Its

The newly completed Tay Bridge.

designer, Sir Thomas Bouch, had been knighted by Queen Victoria after she crossed the bridge in July 1879. The queen had exulted at the view from her carriage as it made its way far above the river. Ulysses S. Grant, the former American president, also celebrated the bridge while visiting Scotland that same year. All this attention thrilled the British public, who cherished their country's reputation of having the greatest engineers in the world.

The bridge consisted of seventy-two spans of deck trusses, where the railway track ran on top of the span, and, at the highest point of the crossing, thirteen through-trusses, where the track ran inside the steel structure. Although truss bridges usually have a very muscular appearance with columns and cross-bracing, the great length of the Tay Bridge made it seem almost feathery, as if it floated above the river. Publicity at the opening of the bridge had brought thousands of tourists north from Edinburgh who wanted to cross the bridge themselves. But not as many did so now, more than a year later and in the dead of winter.

FATEFUL CHOICES

Most people thought the bridge remarkable, although some critics at the time thought it was lacking in substance, its towers (the cast-iron columns that supported the trusses) too narrow at the base to properly brace against the heavy wind loads brought to bear against the bridge. Many people living north of the river had used the bridge frequently after its opening, but some had gone back to the ferries because of disturbing movements within the structure of the bridge as heavy trains passed over it. Some reported a wave-like motion as the trains crossed from pier to pier. Others said the bridge rattled and shook from side to side, particularly when trains passed through the trusses at the highest point in the crossing. The swaying and rattling were even worse when the locomotive engineers exceeded the speed limit of twenty-five miles per hour, which they did frequently when trying to make up for time lost waiting to cross the single track across the river. Painters who maintained the bridge were disturbed to find cracks of up to six feet in length in some of the heavy cast-iron columns that supported the tallest towers. And hundreds of broken lugs were scattered on the caissons at the base of the towers, caused by a faulty design in the columns themselves. The lugs were essential to keep the cross-braces in tension (pulling together), so each failure left the columns weakened.

Good maintenance could have corrected many of those problems, but the British North Railway had delegated maintenance to the designer, Sir Thomas Bouch, who only made infrequent visits to the bridge to check on its integrity. He was busy working on plans to build an even larger bridge across the Firth of Forth, north of Edinburgh. Bouch delegated the task of maintaining the Tay Bridge to Henry Noble, who had assisted in building the masonry footings of the bridge. While Noble was skilled in masonry, he had no experience in ironworks. So when he noticed gaps appearing in the joints between the iron columns and crossties, he simply put shims in the gaps to quiet the rattling. This made the bridge incredibly unsafe since it meant that the crossties were no longer in tension, which caused the bridge to lose strength and coherence. As one crosstie failed, greater stress was placed on adjoining crossties, which added to the strain on the already deficient lugs, leading to even more cracks and failures.

Another decision, a few months earlier, had made the bridge even less steady. At Sir Thomas's direction, 36,000 pounds of stone ballast had been added to the high trusses to reduce the risk of fire from sparks and cinders dropping on the heavy wooden railroad ties. This additional weight raised the bridge's center of gravity, leaving it even more top-heavy on the narrow towers that supported it.

Still, the bridge had held up to thousands of crossings and, as most people do, the passengers on the trains had come to accept it as a permanent fixture in their travels between Edinburgh, Dundee, and Aberdeen. The bridge shortened their travel time by many hours. And, after all, if you couldn't trust the British North Railway, who could you trust?

THE EDINBURGH EXPRESS—DECEMBER 28, 1879

Thirty-seven-year-old locomotive engineer David Mitchell left his wife, Janet, and their four young children at home in Dundee at 5:30 A.M., so he could prepare for the round-trip journey between Dundee and Edinburgh to the south. He and his fireman, John Marshall, a twenty-four-year-old bachelor, would drive the train south in the morning and return over the same route that evening. Theirs would be the first and the last to cross the Tay Bridge on this cold Sunday in December.

The Edinburgh Express needed to depart precisely at 7:30 A.M. David Mitchell was not usually assigned to the Sunday train, but he had traded his shift with another engineer, William Walker, so Mitchell could attend a family event. This was repayment for Walker's kindness. Reaching the engine shed just before 6:00 A.M., he was joined by fireman John Marshall. They would spend the next hour and a half preparing for the journey south. The fire had to be built up, steam raised, and all the fittings checked and cleaned to assure safe passage. Steam engines in 1879 were kept gleaming, despite the coal dust, their brass fittings and green enameled surfaces washed and polished before every trip.

Engine No. 224 was assigned to this train. It was a large steam locomotive for the time, weighing more than thirty-seven tons when filled with coal and water. The driving wheels were six feet in diameter. The rest of the train consisted of a large tender that held three tons of coal and 1,650 gallons of water,[1] as well as five passenger carriages and a guard van (caboose) for the conductor and brakeman. All but one of the cars was equipped with the new American-made Westinghouse brake system, which used heavy springs to keep the brakes applied *unless* air pressure was present to lift them from the wheels. This meant that if the engine ever lost power or any car became uncoupled, the brakes would automatically close and bring the train to a stop. The wheels on every car were also inspected before each journey by using a hammer to tap each wheel to listen for irregularities. Several years earlier, a train had a wheel crack while in transit at high speeds, and the resulting accident had killed many on board. So, Mitchell and Marshall applied the test to each and every wheel. By the scheduled time of departure, all was in order.

The Edinburgh Express was the first to the Tay Bridge and, aside from the usual swaying and clattering, the crossing was uneventful. The two-hour morning trip down to the north shore of the Firth of Forth at Burntisland was uneventful. Most of the passengers made their way from the Burntisland station to Edinburgh by ferry.

Because only two trains operated on Sunday, rather than the usual eight on weekdays, the crew had to endure an eight-hour layover. While much of that time was spent again checking the wheels and preparing for the return trip north to Dundee, there was still time for the crew to nap, read, or play cards.

The weather was quite normal for a midwinter day until late afternoon. But by 5:27 P.M., when the train left the Burntisland station, the barometer had dropped precipitously, particularly at the Dundee end of the line. With sunset at 3:41 P.M. in that far northern district, the entire journey would be made in darkness. Still, Mitchell and Marshall expected to be home by 8:00 P.M. and so did the seventy-five passengers who were on the train as it reached the last station before the Tay Bridge.

The weather was concerning. The icy blasts of the North Sea storm buffeted the station and caused the train carriages to rock back and forth on the track. Some of the passengers were nervous about proceeding in such violent gales. To ease their fears, they had jokingly asked the stationmaster if it was safe to cross the bridge that night, or if the heavy gale would blow the train off the tracks. They had reason to be nervous. On the Royal Navy ship HMS *Mars*,[2] anchored in the Tay River just upstream from the bridge, the officer of the deck logged wind gales between force 10 (55–63 mph) and force

11 (64–72 mph) on the Beaufort scale, which tops out at force 12 (hurricane-force winds over 72 mph). Many of the younger members of the crew confessed that it was terrifying to experience such winds even at anchor. What was particularly disconcerting was that the gusts of up to seventy-five miles per hour were followed by disarmingly peaceful lulls until the next blow. The contrast accentuated the force of the wind when the next blast hit.

Still, everyone on the train was anxious to go home, though an earlier train was seen to create a shower of sparks as the right flanges of the train wheels were driven hard against the iron rails each time a gust hit the train while on the bridge. That was a sign that the cars were being pushed hard against the rails, but not enough to turn them over. One of the guards on that earlier train reportedly went up to the engineer after the crossing and said, "I'd not go across the bridge again tonight for a bonus of £500.[3] My coach was lifted from the rails and streaks of fire came from it."[4]

That was the state of affairs as engineer Mitchell prepared to move the Edinburgh Express onto the bridge in the darkness. The passengers on the train varied from well-dressed businessmen to workingmen with their wives and children. Most had been south to visit family and were returning home for work on Monday. All were defying the religious ministers who said it was a sin to travel on Sunday.

In all, there were approximately seventy passengers. Children weren't ticketed, so the exact number was unknown. There were also five members of the train crew as it started its way onto the bridge at 7:30 P.M. The winds howled as it encountered the first of the deck trusses. In good weather it took just five or six minutes to cross the bridge to the Dundee station.

Interestingly, people on both sides of the river followed the progress of the train in the darkness. Some observers had family on board and were anxious about their arrival. Others were out in the storm trying to tie down valued objects, but curious at the sight of the sparks coming from the train as it mounted ever higher into the sky.

There was a bright moon that evening, which was sometimes obscured by the clouds and then suddenly exposed to the sky and river when the clouds separated. Each time it shone, the bridge was revealed in ghostly silhouette. The train was too small to see clearly at a distance, so most observers followed its progress by the light of the lanterns on the engine at the front of the train and on the guard van at the rear of the train. The Edinburgh Express's progress could also be followed by the showers of sparks from the wheels whenever a gust of wind blew against the carriages.

No one knows what it felt like to be on the train as it reached the zenith of the crossing. What is known is that just as it reached the highest point of the bridge, a particularly violent gust of wind struck the bridge with hurricane force. Observers noted that it was 7:15 P.M., and it was a blast unlike anything the storm had yet given that night. One can imagine that the bridge was chattering and swaying from the combined weight of 288 tons of bridgework plus 113 tons of train perched precariously on top of the slender iron towers. The wind load was already straining the bridge when that blast hit full force, and it created an additional stress that proved too much to resist:

"Shortly after seven o'clock they saw the lights of the train as it entered upon the bridge, a dim, uncertain glimmer far away. Alexander watched the signal light to the north of the High Girders. It was flickering and he wondered if the lamp had set fire to its mounting. Then he took his eyes from it and watched the approach of the train. He watched until it entered the High Girders and then he saw one, two, three great flashes of light that lasted long enough for him to see the fretwork of iron, or think he saw it. It was his opinion that these flashes occurred in front of the train, and he always maintained that this was so.

"William Millar, however, believed that the flashes came from the train itself, and when he saw them, he turned to his friends and said jocularly that the fireman must be in a hurry to get home for he was drawing his fire already, and was throwing the coals into the river.

"It was not easy to see anything with great certainty, for one moment there would be a scud of cloud across the moon and the next moment the scene would be clear in the pallid light. William stood up and moved close to the window. He saw a white flash against the bridge. 'They're blowing steam, now,' he said, and scarcely had he said this than he shouted in a vastly altered tone, 'The bridge is down!'"[5]

It was almost too fantastic to believe. Yet dozens of people saw the same sequence of events from numerous vantage points. The train was passing over the bridge at a good clip, sparks lighting up the night sky each time a blast of wind struck the carriages. Observers knew when it entered the high girders because the headlamp seemed to flicker as the beams of the trusses came between the train and the observers. Then the train disappeared for a few moments, perhaps five seconds, followed by three bright flashes, forward of where the train should have been. This was followed by two large columns of water shooting up from the river and then cascading back down. Observers also reported an indistinct mist from the northern end of the spot where the train was supposed to exit the through-trusses.

Then there was darkness and silence.

THE BRIDGE IS DOWN!

Some people rubbed their eyes. Others refused to believe their eyes. A few started shouting, "The bridge is down!" as they ran towards the river. Those with telescopes trained them on the bridge, but the moon was once again hidden behind the clouds. When it finally broke clear, there was nothing but empty space in the air above twelve empty caissons, standing like stumps in the river. Waves crashing against the caissons' upstream face revealed their place in the water. Worse, there was nothing showing in the river to suggest that a massive iron bridge and train had been there moments before.

As word of the disaster spread, people started to congregate at the base of the bridge and at the railway station. With the storm howling and the clouds often throwing the scene into blackness, all sorts of stories started circulating. Some said the bridge was down, but that the train had stopped before it collapsed. Others said the bridge was still there, but the train had decided to back down to the south shore because of the gale. Still another ran up to say that the train was "off the bridge" but not that the bridge itself had collapsed.

At the Dundee train station, stationmaster James Smith tried to make sense of the conflicting reports flooding in. While he didn't know what had happened to the train or the bridge, he did know that the telegraph line to the south bank was inoperative. This suggested that something had cut the line. He also knew that the Edinburgh Express was thirty minutes late, which was unheard of given the time it should have taken to cross the bridge. Anxious to know the truth, he and British North Railway engineer James Roberts decided to find out what had or had not happened. They started walking out on the bridge to find the missing train, but Smith hesitated in the heavy winds, so Roberts continued alone:

"Roberts resolutely persisted alone into the nightmare of the storm. Eventually, although it must have seemed to him like forever and more, he reached the end of the low spans. He should have been able to see the high girders looming above him into the night sky but there was nothing. Crawling to within about [eight yards] of the last standing span he saw the gap. There were no high girders left, just nothingness. . . . Roberts could see that the broken-off rails weren't twisted, just bent downwards. A huge jet of water was spurting from the severed end of the Newport water main and the ebbing tide was certainly swirling on something just below the water."[6]

That was a sight never to be forgotten: almost ninety feet above the frothing River Tay, at the edge of a bridge that ended abruptly, with rails twisted straight down towards the water. The pipe that was

The aftermath of the bridge's collapse.

shooting a spray of water into the air carried fresh water from the north shore to the south; its break was the cause of the mist reported by observers on the shore. The three flashes reported by observers were caused by either sparks from the iron girders being torn apart as the columns collapsed, or from gas explosions from the natural gas line that fed the lights on the bridge.

The most likely sequence of events went like this:

As the unusually strong blast hit the bridge with hurricane force, it created fatal stress on the high girders at the rear of the train. This initiated a slow-motion, rolling collapse from one pier to the next as the roadbed dragged down each pier in the line. Eyewitness accounts established that it took a full ten seconds to topple the other through-truss sections in a domino style from south to north.

The guard van at the rear of the train was the first to start falling. The passengers in cars forward of the guard van likely became aware of the problem as the train was jerked from behind, its forward motion reversing abruptly as the cars were pulled down from behind. The failing bridge would have created an incredible increase in the ambient noise as metal beams and columns started popping, tearing, and crashing against each other. When added to the noise of the gale-force winds, it had to have been a cacophony of earsplitting sound that assaulted the humans on the train.

With the wind blowing against the western side of the carriages, the bridge fell to the east, downstream and to the right-hand side of the train when facing forward. In turn, the cars started tipping to the right at the same moment they began falling backward, down toward the river, tumbling their terrified occupants around their compartments as the train fell. Worse, the train cars were now locked inside the massive through-trusses, which were also falling. This made it impossible for any air trapped inside the carriages to bring them to the surface after hitting the water.

So great was the force of the train's collision with the water that some cars literally exploded, their roofs blown right off. Lighter-weight cars disintegrated, while heavier cars immediately filled with water and quickly disappeared under the waves, dragged down by the bridge that now surrounded them. Passengers and crew in the carriages had no time to escape as they were plunged into freezing water immediately after being stunned by the impact with the water.

In other words, the bridge's failure and the train falling into the river left more than enough time for the train's passengers to be very much aware of what was happening to them, but with no hope of escape.

VICTIMS AND
FIRST-RESPONDER HEROES

Organizing a rescue mission out into the water proved difficult. First, it took a great deal of time to simply figure out what had happened and where the train had gone. Second, the tide was ebbing (moving out to sea), which lowered the river's level to the point that many larger steamboats couldn't maneuver to the bridge site. And finally, there was the storm, which was still raging, making it extremely dangerous for small boats to venture out into the windswept waves.

Finally, by 10:00 P.M., the river had calmed enough for the steam-powered ferryboat *Dundee* to leave shore. It took the captain

An illustration of the rescue and recovery attempts after the Tay Bridge collapse.

an hour to maneuver the boat in a wide arc downstream from the fallen bridge while avoiding sandbars in the ebb tide. He was fighting a strong current as he drew near the bridge's foundation caissons. Rather than risk damaging the ferryboat, he assembled a qualified crew and dispatched them in a rowboat to see if they could find any survivors struggling in the water. Occasionally someone shouted out that they saw a human form, but it always turned out to be a piece of wood from the collapsed railroad ties.

After searching for more than an hour, the would-be rescuers reluctantly abandoned the effort. It was now three and a half hours since the bridge had failed, and they understood that no one could remain alive after that long in thirty-four-degree (Fahrenheit) water. The ferry recovered its rescue boat and steamed to shore. Some on board were hopeful that some passengers had managed to swim to shore downstream and that they would be found safe the next morning. But their hopes were in vain. Some debris, including mail bags, washed up on the northern shore, but not a single survivor.

The next day, more boats went out into the river, still hoping to find someone clinging to one of the twelve stumps that had earlier supported the towers. But there was no one. A diver attempted to find the bridge under the surface, but the river was too turgid from the storm for him to see anything. Eventually, the jagged end of a cast-iron beam was spotted sticking up at an angle above the water. Here was proof that the bridge lay beneath the waves.

Despite the heroic efforts of the men who braved the stormy river, placing their own lives at risk, no survivors were found.

The first victim was found later that day, December 29, 1879, on the downstream shore. Her name was Ann Cruikshank, a maid. Other bodies emerged a few days later downstream from the wreck, a process which continued gradually for several months. Fewer than half of the bodies of the passengers and crew were eventually recovered, leaving thirty-nine unaccounted for.

The railroad locomotive was also found on December 29 and was eventually raised from the riverbed, although it fell back into the river two times during the salvage attempts. Once recovered, it was found to be remarkably undamaged and was successfully refurbished and placed back into service. Later engineers called it "the Diver" because of its three plunges into the river. It was telling that the steam regulator (throttle) had not been reduced, nor the brakes applied. In other words, engineer David Mitchell apparently had no

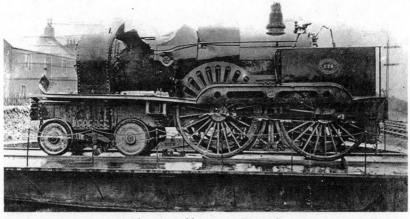

The recovered locomotive (No. 224).

warning of the disaster unfolding beneath and behind him, so the train simply charged ahead as it fell. The wheels would have started spinning at a high rate of speed as soon as the tracks fell away below them, but there would have been no time to react. The body of fireman John Marshall was found wedged under a load of coal, his face pressed against the burning hot footplate. His agony started before the others, as his body was burned by the 800-degree plate before the locomotive splashed into the river.[7]

Of course, there were more victims than those who lost their lives. Janet Mitchell became a widow, and her children became fatherless. As there was not a single surviving passenger, the family and friends of at least seventy-five people were devastated by the death of a loved one. Almost half of the family and friends affected were never able to lay to rest the body of their loved one.

PROFESSIONAL HEROES—ACTING TO PREVENT FUTURE TRAGEDY

A STORY HEARD ROUND THE WORLD

Reporters for the Dundee-area newspapers learned of the tragedy as it first unfolded. They immediately began writing up the story and transmitting it by telegraph using lines that went upstream to the town of Perth, west of the estuary. The telegraph lines from the collapsed bridge were among the first remnants found by divers when the river finally quieted down. One of the first people to respond to the newspaper reports was Queen Victoria, who was horrified at the loss of life on a railroad line that she had personally celebrated just five months earlier. As word reached London, the story was posted via transatlantic cable to America. Soon the whole world knew about the failure of the famous Tay Bridge. At first it was reported that more than three hundred people had perished, the usual number of riders on the Edinburgh Express. But once it was remembered that it had been a Sunday evening train, the estimate fell quickly to seventy-five, although there may have been a few more.

WHY DID THE BRIDGE FAIL?

The horror and pity of the crowds quickly turned to rage. They demanded to know why the bridge had failed, hurling the question at the British North Railway and its famous designer, Sir Thomas Bouch. Bouch was awakened on the night of the collapse and agreed to join BNR officials on a railcar to the south shore of the River Tay. A day earlier he had been considered a genius. Now he was met with anger. A court of inquiry was convened, with leading engineers of the day sitting in judgment to determine the cause of the failure and what should be done to prevent a similar failure in the future.

After examining the wreckage of the bridge and the recovered train carriages, Bouch argued that the wind had blown one of the carriages off its track, and when it had struck a beam in the high girders, the bridge had failed. In his opinion, it had been an act of God, the wind bringing the bridge down, not the bridge failing. His theory was immediately met with derision. Even if it were true, how was it possible that Bouch had designed a bridge so fragile that damage to one beam out of thousands could pull down the whole structure? His reputation was destroyed.

The inquiry called dozens of witnesses, including those who could provide an eyewitness account of the tragedy, eminent engineers, foundrymen who had cast the iron, workers who had built the bridge, and others who had maintained it. They even called on painters who had worked on the bridge as trains passed through. The story that emerged was one of incompetence of design and maintenance.

After weeks of testimony and on-site inspections, the conclusion was that while the severe winds of December 28, 1879, played some part in bringing the bridge down that specific night, it was inevitable that the bridge would fail because of multiple deficiencies

The ruins of the Tay Bridge.

that included an inadequate design of both the base and the towers that supported the superstructure. The narrow footprint of the towers relative to the bridge's weight was like a person trying to balance on one foot, rather than on two feet spread apart, which would provide maximum stability.

Another deficiency was poor workmanship in the casting of the iron columns that supported the bridge. The Wormit ironworks had certified that they had provided their "best" grade of iron. What wasn't mentioned until the court of inquiry is that they had three grades: "best," "best-best," and "best-best-best." The iron used in the bridge was actually the lowest grade. Some of the problems with the casting included using sand from the Tay River, which was infused with saltwater, rather than pure sand that would not adversely affect the steel. The casting process was also poorly supervised, leading to large variances in the thickness of the column walls. It also led to "blow-holes," which occurred when gases, trapped in the metal while it cooled, left weak spots or holes in the column that compromised its integrity. Rather than recasting such columns, these were sometimes filled with cement or wax to make it appear as if the columns were whole. These defects in the already poor-quality iron led to six-foot cracks in the columns. Bouch's answer to cracked columns, when they were found, was to wrap them rather than replace them. Many felt that Bouch had chosen the Wormit foundry over others because of a personal connection to its owner, despite its reputation for shoddy work.

Yet another deficiency was the poor design of the "lugs" that extruded from the iron columns and to which the crossties were attached. The best practice of the day was to cast the column continuously, and to then drill holes in the column and attach the crossties with separately made wrought-iron lugs. In the Tay Bridge, the lugs were cast as part of the column itself, which meant that they were subject to cracking and breaking. An even more serious problem was that when the casting process failed to fully form a lug, the workaround was to "burn one on," welding a piece of cast iron to the column. This shortcut would result in a lug even less able to bear the tension load. The failure of hundreds of lugs prior to the night of the collapse had taken more and more of the tie-bars out of tension, leaving the already narrow towers without the tension necessary to hold them together in their strongest configuration.

Another failure came from bolts too small for the loads placed on them, and conical holes in the iron that did not allow the bolts to be fully tightened. The thousands of trains that had passed over the bridge in its nineteen-month lifespan had loosened many bolts that were supposed to maintain structural integrity. This contributed to movement in the towers, the swaying and rattling that had been reported by painters as heavy trains crossed over.

Another design failure was that the girders rested directly on the towers, rather than connecting through plates that would have more evenly distributed the load.

Sir Thomas Bosch had also made no allowance for wind loads in his design of the bridge. In both France and the United States, structures of this type were required to withstand wind gusts of up to fifty pounds per square foot. Since no other major structures in the vicinity collapsed the night of December 28, including smokestacks, railroad buildings, or even house chimneys, the bridge should have also resisted the wind load. Multiple loose-fitting joints and tie-bars had increased its susceptibility to the wind, which increased the danger when the wind struck the train at the very top of the bridge structure.

Sir Thomas's design of the towers consisted of two hexagonal columns that were not tied together at the top where the truss-work rested. In other words, it was like having two legs not connected to each other. This substantially reduced the structural integrity of the towers themselves. This serious flaw was discovered in the wreckage after the collapse. The court of inquiry clearly showed that the eastern columns had failed first, followed by the trusses dropping, then the collapse of the western columns. Had the paired towers been held together by a ring at the top, they would have acted as one, allowing the western columns to lend strength to the eastern columns, which were under increased strain from the wind.

In Sir Thomas's design, the substantial weight of the superstructure was also out of balance with the supporting towers, which put the center of gravity almost at the top of the through-trusses. Like standing while holding a weight over your head in a strong wind: even slight lateral movements could lead to toppling, which is exactly what happened on the night of the collapse.

And then other factors contributed, including excessive train speeds. Many trains were observed to travel faster than the posted twenty-five-mile-per-hour speed limit. The faster a train went, the greater the vibrations in the bridge and corresponding increase in stress on the joints, bolts, and lugs.

Poor maintenance was also a factor. Despite continuing reports of motion and chattering in the bridge, no steps were taken to remedy the defects. In fact, the use of shims to quiet the rattling diminished the strength of the towers while giving the false appearance of having solved the problem.

There is much more from a technical perspective that describes the causes of the failure, but these were the most important failings of the bridge. At the end of the inquiry, the three commissioners were unanimous in their judgment:

"The conclusion then, to which we have come, is that this bridge was badly designed, badly constructed and badly maintained, and that its downfall was due to inherent defects in the structure, which must sooner or later have brought it down. For these defects both in the design, the construction and the maintenance, Sir Thomas Bouch is, in our opinion, mainly to blame. For the faults of design he is entirely responsible. For those of construction he is principally to blame in not having exercised that supervision over the work, which would have enabled him to detect and apply a remedy to them. And for the faults of maintenance he is also principally, if not entirely, to blame in having neglected to maintain such an inspection over the structure, as its character imperatively demanded."[8]

This was a damning analysis for Sir Thomas Bouch. Those who wished to defend him pointed out that there was no requirement at the time for calculating wind loads or incorporating them into the design. But people of the day knew better. When the report was released to the public on July 3, 1880, the London *Times* noted that the inspection routine was wholly inadequate. While it did test for vertical loads (gravity), it did not test for lateral loads (wind and swaying). The newspaper concluded that the bridge had never been safe and was destined to fail from the day it was put into service.

Others who wished to defend Bouch pointed out that a bridge of this length and scale had never been attempted before, which suggested that it was beyond the engineering of the day. However, the replacement Tay Bridge, built on entirely new foundations just a few yards upstream of the Bouch bridge, was completed in 1887 and is still in service today, more than one hundred and thirty years later. Clearly, the engineering of the day was adequate to build a bridge equal to the challenge, if properly designed and maintained.

Many historical accounts suggest that Sir Thomas Bouch was demoralized by the collapse of the bridge and the subsequent inquiry, even though no criminal responsibility was assigned. That he died just ten months after the failure adds to this impression. But contemporary reports from the time, of his activities both during and after the inquiry, suggested that he was not the type of man to feel any personal guilt or responsibility for what had happened.

In fact, he was busy designing the replacement bridge while the inquiry was still taking place, fully confident of his ability to replace the lost sections. He also worked on the design of a suspension bridge across the Firth of Forth at Edinburgh, with the full support of the British North Railway. But the public would not have it. Public uproar and disgust at the idea of Bouch building other bridges was too much for the company to bear and so, apologetically, they cancelled their contract with Bouch. But he had other projects he wanted to pursue and was doing so when he died. Even though declared incompetent as an engineer, he continued to work as if nothing had happened.

New Engineering Safety Standards

A five-member "Wind Pressure on Railway Structures" Select Committee was set up by Parliament immediately after the release of the report from the inquiry's commissioners. The select committee's specific tasks were to study the effect of wind loads on bridges and towers, and to develop standards to protect against their effects. They set up numerous monitoring stations all through Great Britain, and collected reports from Europe and the United States. The highest recorded pressure they encountered was 65.6 pounds per square foot. Sir Thomas Bouch had assumed a wind load of 10 pounds per square foot in designing the first Tay Bridge, and so had made no allowance for wind loads at all, since he assumed the effect was negligible. The committee settled on a figure of 56.6 pounds per square foot as the minimum standard (with a safety factor of two) to which bridges in the UK should be designed thereafter. In addition, engineers took note of the other deficiencies noted in the inquiry and adjusted to compensate for the failings. One of the newest innovations was to substitute steel for cast or wrought iron, with a significant increase in strength and flexibility.

When these regulations were put into effect, many existing structures were either retrofitted or taken down because it was clear they were not in compliance. One bridge that was destroyed before it was even put into service was the very last structure designed by Sir Thomas Bouch, built by his son after his father's death. Virtually all the mistakes made in the Tay Railway Bridge had been repeated in this new structure, even though it was designed *after* the collapse. Bouch was both stubborn and unteachable.

CONCLUSION

More than seventy-five lives were lost that stormy December night in 1879, including a young father who piloted the train to its fate. It was not his regular shift; he had traded with another man who was safe at home when the Tay Bridge collapsed. David Mitchell and his passengers and fellow crewmembers lost their lives to Sir Thomas Bouch's incompetence and hubris. But because of their loss, millions have traveled in greater safety across hundreds of thousands of bridges around the globe.

CHAPTER 3

1906: HARRIMAN FIGHTS THE COLORADO

THE HUMAN COST OF TRAGEDY

It had seemed like a pipe dream for decades, but at the dawn of the twentieth century, new tools, capital, and political will combined to make irrigating the Imperial Valley in Southern California a reality. It was a gigantic mistake. Nearly immediately, the canals began to fill with sediment. Then the developers responsible, faced with financial ruin, made an even more colossal mistake: making yet another diversion, called the "Mexican Cut," and installing a temporary headgate that, partially because of where it was installed and partially because of particularly heavy rains, soon breached, unleashing a raging torrent that carried most of the Colorado River into the Salton Sink, an arid depression, turning it into the Salton Sea, nearly 350 square miles of water with no natural outlet.

Witnesses described the great flood as "a raging torrent of huge waterfalls" up to a thousand feet wide and eighty feet high.[1] Soil along the cut was eroding at the rate of one foot per second. Author Marc Reisner related, "Even as their fields were being eaten and as their homes swam away, the valley people came out by the hundreds to see this apparition, a twenty-foot falls moving backward at a slow walk."[2] And "Henry Thomas Cory, the engineer largely responsible for finally containing the flood, estimated that the volume of earth washed down into the Salton Sink during nine months of flooding equaled four times the amount excavated during construction of the Panama Canal."[3]

"After two years of successive flooding" in which the mighty Colorado River poured billions of gallons of water into the Imperial Valley south of Palm Springs, California, thousands of acres of fertile farm land was either left high and dry after the river washed out the canals and headgates that irrigated their crops, or the land was "completely ravaged with much of it underwater."[4] More than 2,000 farmers watched helplessly as their life savings evaporated along with the water no longer available to their parched crops. Economic disaster, including the threat of starvation, loomed in their future from a fully preventable man-made tragedy of unequaled scale. The finest engineers of the day seemed helpless in finding a solution to the floods that threatened to fill the ancient sink and destroy all the residents' hopes and dreams. But there was one man—just one—with the courage, foresight, and financial resources to mount a fight against the Colorado River and perhaps arrest the tragedy that was growing in scope and danger every single day. Even with battle lines drawn, the outcome was anything but certain, and the cost would reach historic proportions. All because of a desperate gamble gone wrong.

OVERVIEW

Two-thirds of the fresh vegetables eaten in the United States in winter are grown in the Imperial Valley of California. The climate and soil are so perfectly matched that virtually anything can grow there, often yielding three or four crops per season. More than one hundred varieties of fruit and grains are planted on half a million acres of irrigated farmland there, including such exotic crops as

A map of the area of the All-American Canal.

bamboo, sugar cane, flax, artichokes, cilantro, and water lilies—and staples like corn, carrots, and lettuce. It is the cornucopia of America. If you've ever eaten a salad in winter, you've been fed by the farmers of the Imperial Valley.

Beautiful date palm trees line the boulevards of the valley's major cities, including Palm Springs, Indio, Coachella, and El Centro. The valley's verdant green fields are a delight to the eye amid the otherwise brown and barren desert sand. This lush oasis is made green by the waters of the formidable Colorado River.

THE GREAT COLORADO DESERT

In the year 1540, a Spanish explorer named Melchior Diaz reached the edge of the great Salton Sink, in which the Imperial Valley is located. Diaz saw nothing but a fierce arid desert with less than three inches of rainfall per year and unbearably hot summer temperatures. It was a forlorn area.

The eastern slopes of the valley border the Algodones sand

dunes, an almost otherworldly setting that has delighted movie directors for decades, perhaps best known for portraying the desert planet Tatooine in George Lucas's *Return of the Jedi*, acres of rippling sand baking in sun so hot that nothing grows. Diaz reported back to his commander, Francisco Vásquez de Coronado, that there was nothing of value in that part of California. The area was left undisturbed by humans for another 300 years.

But all that was needed to turn the Salton Sink into the Imperial Valley was water. For visionaries in the late 1800s, the answer was obvious—divert a portion of the Colorado River into the Salton Sink, using gravity to feed a network of canals. It sounded farfetched to some, but the Colorado River had emptied into the sink for extended periods deep into the geologic record. At one point in geologic time, the sink was filled with water and connected to the Gulf of California at the south. But 3,000 years ago, silt[5] from the Colorado River filled the channel leading into the lake. The Colorado River now runs due south of Yuma, Arizona, into Mexico and on to the Gulf of California, bypassing the Salton Sink.

As the water in the ancient lake dried up, it left the Salton Sink as its remnant, a desolate bowl 300 feet below sea level and 400 feet below the Colorado River to the east.

The Idea of a Colorado River Canal Is Born

Several entrepreneurs had thought of building a canal from the Colorado River into the Sink in the late 1800s, but the engineering challenges were too daunting. For one, it was thought that the hot desert climate—which routinely hit 120 degrees (Fahrenheit) and had been recorded as high as 150 degrees in the summer—was too inhospitable for humans to work in over extended periods of time.

In 1901, an eminent water engineer from Los Angeles, George M. Chaffey, became interested in the project after completing an irrigation project in similar temperatures in central Australia. What the sponsors of that project had learned was that people can work and live in high temperatures if the humidity is low. One characteristic of arid deserts is that the temperature falls quickly at night when the sun goes down. Perhaps most important to Chaffey was that average temperatures in winter in the Salton Sink area were in the 70s.

With the question of habitability settled, Chaffey put up his own money to fund the project through a new company, the California Development Company and its Mexican subsidiary.

THE ALAMO CANAL AND
THE IMPERIAL LAND COMPANY

A series of hills west of the Colorado River at Yuma made it difficult to build a canal to the Salton Sink north of the Mexico–United States border. But further to the south, the hills tapered off just inside Mexico, and a series of washes provided a natural path to the southern end of the Imperial Valley, utilizing the streambed of the usually dry Alamo River, which only flowed during high floods on the lower Colorado, feeding water into the Salton Sink. Once agreements were secured with the Mexican government, workers began excavating a fourteen-mile canal that started with headgates in the United States and then headed south into Mexico to connect with the dry streambed of the Alamo River. In May 1901, water began flowing into the Alamo Canal. For the first time in history, water left the Colorado River for the Salton Sink as a result of human intervention. The canal had a capacity to deliver up to 400,000 acre-feet of water per year.

With ample water secured, the next step in the plan was to attract farmers to the area. Thinking that the area's historic name, "the Great Colorado Desert," wouldn't sound too appealing, the promoters christened the area "the Imperial Valley." They formed the Imperial Land Company in 1901 and began selling interests to Eastern investors. The new name was successful in attracting farmers and just one year later, 400 miles of irrigation ditches had been dug to draw water from the canal. This opened more than 100,000 acres to farming and was a roaring success. By 1904, more than ten thousand settlers had moved into the region and the Southern Pacific Railroad had built railroad lines into the valley to carry out the abundant, year-round produce:

"Grapes, melons and garden vegetables matured in the Valley earlier than in any other part of California; barley was a profitable crop; alfalfa could be cut five or six times a year; and the finest quality of long-staple Egyptian cotton yielded more than a bale (five hundred pounds) to the acre. Experiments also proved that the climate and soil were well-adapted to the culture of grapes, grapefruit, oranges, lemons, olives, figs, dates, pomegranates, apricots, peaches, and pears."[6]

George Chaffey's predictions for the valley had proven true. But then nature intervened to imperil the livelihood of the new residents.

FATEFUL CHOICES

SILT, DRIFTING SAND, AND A RECKLESS CUT IN THE RIVER

A single day of water for the Imperial Valley contained enough silt to create a levee twenty feet high, twenty feet wide, and a mile long—a single day! Right from the beginning, the biggest problem the canal company faced was silt clogging the headgates of the canal and depositing sediment in the canals. It was a constant battle to keep water flowing, even as demand for water increased because of new arrivals. The problem become critical in 1904, when the first four miles of the canal filled with so much sediment that almost no water got through. Crops burned up in the fields and damage claims exceeding half a million dollars (equivalent to $13 million in 2019 dollars) were filed by farmers against the canal company, nearly driving the young company to bankruptcy. Because they lacked equipment to dredge the canal, the chief engineer, C. R. Rockwood,

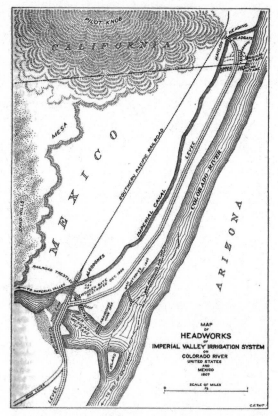

A contemporary map of the Imperial Valley irrigation system.

directed his employees to cut a new entrance to the canal four miles south of the Mexican border, to simply bypass the silted-up channel.

Because time was of the essence, Rockwood chose not to build concrete headgates; the company simply cut through the riverbank to allow water to start flowing immediately. It was the beginning of winter, which had the lowest river flows of the year, so it seemed a low-risk operation. The farmers were in favor, as it would provide them immediate relief. Everyone involved recognized that it was crucial that permanent headgates be installed before the usual summer floods hit, to prevent an uncontrolled flood into the canals. Plans were drawn up and submitted to the Mexican government for approval.

After what looked like a successful solution to the problem, the Colorado had an unpleasant surprise in store—three, in fact. There had been a winter flood in only three of the previous twenty-seven years, and those had been moderate. In the winter of 1905, the Colorado sent three major floods cascading down its channel. The first two carried such a heavy silt load that they clogged up the new cut, requiring more dredging. Two floods in quick succession signaled that it was an unusual year, so the operators decided to close up the unprotected cut and reuse the headgates upstream in advance of the summer flood season. In March 1905, they began closing the cut. Then the Colorado sent a *third* winter flood, something that had never been observed. This flood washed out the temporary closing of the cut and sent much of the increased river flow directly into the Alamo canal, which now had far more water than the canal network was designed to handle.

A second attempt to close the cut two weeks later was also swept away. By June 1905, the Colorado was pouring 90,000 cubic feet of water per second (cfs) into the opening that had now grown to 160 feet wide. As the water cascaded into the Imperial Valley, it began to deepen the channel of the Alamo River below the level of many of the ditches, cutting off the water supply to the canals and, ultimately, the farms. The only place for the water to go, at that point, was into the very bottom of the Salton Sink, where it began to form a new lake—the lake that today is known as the Salton Sea. This was now a catastrophe in the making. It became increasingly urgent that those responsible close the gap and return the intake to the concrete headgates upstream.

But the canal company had a problem—they were effectively bankrupt and lacked the equipment and manpower to deal with the breach that was now diverting much of the flow of the river.

They tried to borrow money, but the East Coast capital markets were unwilling to make loans on such a risky proposition. So, the canal company turned to the Southern Pacific Railroad with a request for a $200,000 loan. Because of the railroad's stake in transporting Imperial Valley produce to market, it was hoped they would help, but the loan was turned down. As the situation grew

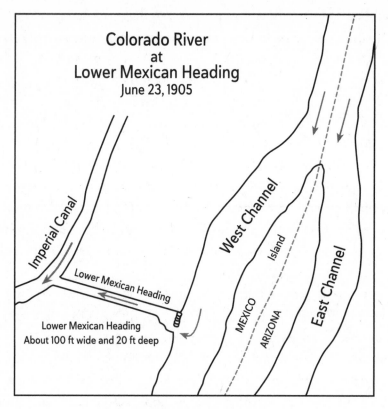

A diagram of the "Mexican Cut."

more urgent, the canal company made an appeal directly to E. H.
Harriman, the president of both the Union Pacific and the Southern
Pacific Railroads. Harriman understood the danger and authorized
the loan, but with the provision that stock in the canal company be
set aside as collateral for repayment of the loan. He also required
that Southern Pacific employees and engineers help solve the problem. It was thought that $20,000 of this loan could close the cut,
and the remainder would be available for other improvements.

By August 1905, the summer floods had passed, and the river
had settled down to approximately 12,000 cfs pouring through
the cut. This should have been the time to act, but Chief Engineer
Rockwood failed to grasp the true gravity of the danger. In fact,
he believed it was a positive development that the flow was scour-
ing out the channel into the Alamo River and sending silt into the

middle of the Salton Sink. What he failed to appreciate was that over the past million years or so, the Colorado had proved itself very willing to change course into the Salton Sink, the last time filling it with the ancient massive lake that had extended to the Gulf of California. There was no reason that such a thing couldn't happen again if the cut deepened to the point that the entire flow of the river was diverted.

Fortunately, Harriman sent his own assistant, H. T. Cory, to survey the scene, and he instantly recognized the danger. By this point in time, Rockwood had tried multiple strategies to close the breach, but without the sense of urgency that was required. For example, he had tried to build a jetty from the western shore of the Colorado out to the island in the middle of the river, thinking that it would force the river away from the opening. This failed, and the jetty breaking increased the amount of water flowing into the breach.

VICTIMS AND FIRST-RESPONDER HEROES

The victims of the Great Flood were the farmers who lost their livelihoods when the canals and headgates were washed out by the water, as well as everyone who had come to depend on Californian fruit and vegetables, from the wholesalers to the grocery stores to the consumers. Fortunately, because there was enough warning, no deaths were attributed to the Colorado floods, although there were injuries among the tens of thousands of men who eventually worked frantically to stanch the flow of the river over multiple attempts and failures. Driving a railroad train out onto a makeshift trestle bridge across a raging river took courage. Operating the heavy equipment that dumped hundreds of thousands of tons of rock and fill into the breach was dangerous and backbreaking.

PROFESSIONAL HEROES—ACTING TO PREVENT FUTURE TRAGEDY

In August, the railroad took direct action to close the breach. The Southern Pacific team assembled a large group of men to end the catastrophe. So great were the cuts in the channel that men risked their lives to venture into the breaches.

Their first attempt was to install a six-hundred-foot brush-mattress and sandbag dam across the opening, at a cost of $60,000. Normally this would have succeeded, but the river had a new surprise: a flood from the Gila River, which begins in Arizona and empties into the Colorado just north of Yuma. Even though the summer flood season was over in the upstream states of the Colorado, the monsoon season in Arizona sent an unexpected flood crashing into the river, increasing the Colorado's flow from 12,000 cfs to 115,000 cfs. This was far more than the makeshift dam could withstand, and it was quickly washed away. The flood also washed out the island in the center of the channel, which meant that the full flow of the river then migrated to the lowest point, which happened to be the six-hundred-foot opening on its western bank. The full flow of the Colorado River was now flooding into the great Salton Sink, destroying the intricate network of canals and ditches that the farmers depended on.

NIAGARA FALLS IN THE COLORADO DESERT

During its high season, Niagara Falls on the United States–Canada border has a total flow of 100,000 cfs over a 164-foot drop. In 1905, the Colorado River was sending almost that much into the new channel it was carving into the ancient Salton Sink. What was most concerning was the high rate of erosion in the soft desert sand, where the floor of the sink was 400 feet lower than the bed of the Colorado River.

As water poured into the valley, it began eroding its way back

Flooding and waterfall caused by the Mexican Cut.

to the main channel. If it wasn't stopped before reaching the mouth of the opening, the Colorado would pour over a 400-foot waterfall that could never be reversed. The canal company was now out of resources and the burden fell entirely on the shoulders of the Southern Pacific Railroad. By summer 1906, the opening to the Alamo River was more than two miles wide.

Mr. Epes Randolph, president of the Arizona and Southern California branches of the Southern Pacific, stepped in to take control of the operation. Chief Engineer Rockwood resigned in disgrace, and H. T. Cory took his place. It would take a total of seven separate actions to finally seal the breach.

Many conflicting plans were put forward to solve the problem, but it was impossible to judge which was best, since no one had ever faced a problem like this before.

Cory was decisive, deciding on a two-pronged approach. First, they would build new headgates upstream from the cut and open a controlled flow into the Alamo channel. That would reduce the flow of water through the cut, allowing them to make repairs. He also initiated a more immediate solution. He ordered the construction of a pile-driven pier that would extend across the opening so that railcars could move across the breach and dump heavy rocks into the opening. It wasn't the first time that a bridge was built over open water,

*Southern Pacific railway cars helping in the effort to block the Colorado River
from flooding into the Salton Sink.*

but it was the first time it was done in such an incredible flow on
such soft and sandy soil. Creating the operation necessary to accomplish this task was very much like going to war. George Kennan, in
his book written just ten years after the event, described it like this:

"President Randolph and his engineers immediately began the
construction of a branch railroad from the main line of the Southern
Pacific to the scene of operations at the crevasse, with ample sid-
ings and terminal facilities at both ends. Then they borrowed from
the Union Pacific three hundred of the mammoth side-dump cars
known as 'battleships,' which . . . had a carrying capacity of fifty or
sixty tons each. The California Development Company had three
light-draught steamers and several barges that could be used on the
river, and the Southern Pacific Company furnished complete work-
trains, from time to time, until a maximum of ten was reached. The
next requisite was material for levees and dams, and this they secured by drawing upon all the rock quarries within a radius of four
hundred miles, and by opening a new one, with a face of six hundred feet and a height of forty feet, on the granite ledge at Andrade
near the concrete head-gate. . . . From Los Angeles they brought
eleven hundred ninety-foot piles, nineteen thousand feet of heavy
timbers for railway trestles, and forty miles of steel cable to be used
in the weaving of brush-mattresses. The Southern Pacific Company

The new river flooding the Imperial Valley, 1907.

furnished pile-drivers, steam shovels for the granite quarry and gravel pit, several carloads of repair parts, and a large quantity of stores and materials of various kinds. It also detailed for service on the spur railroad and at the crevasse as many engineers, mechanics, and skilled workmen as were needed. . . .

"The requisite most difficult to obtain, in sufficient amount, was unskilled labor. . . . Mr. Cory was finally compelled to mobilize all the Indian tribes in that part of the Southwest—Pimas, Papagoes, Maricopas, and Yumas from Arizona and Cocopahs and Diegueños from Mexico. These Indians fraternized and got along together amicably and constituted with their families a separate camp of about two thousand people."[7]

This was a response on an unprecedented scale. The first step—laying down 13,000 square feet of brush-mattress made of baling wire, steel cable, and two thousand cords of brush—took two weeks to accomplish.

The next step was to build the railroad trestle out into the channel: it was ten feet wide and strong enough to support the heavy side-dump "battleships" filled with rock. On September 14, trains started out into the opening, their cars dumping massive amounts of rock into the breach. Simultaneously, the Rockwood gates upstream were completed and opened, and water started flowing into the old channel. This took pressure off the cut, and it looked like success was at hand.

But the level of the river came back up again, destroying the fifth attempt to seal the breach, and destroying the $122,000 two-hundred-foot headgate in the process.

A TEMPORARY VICTORY

Though it's hard to keep track of, there were now three openings to the Imperial Valley from the Colorado River: the original opening that had silted over, the new gates that had been installed north of the cut, and the cut itself. All of these had to be dealt with to finally solve the problem. By November 1905, more than 10,000 carloads of rock had been deposited on the new levee and 400,000 yards of material moved by dredges. It was an unprecedented undertaking, but at long last the breach was sealed, the original canal cleared of silt, and the headgates fully operational. It was an unqualified victory for the Southern Pacific Railroad.

Except that the river was about to make a natural change to the channel, in one final attempt to flood the Imperial Valley.

A NEW PERIL—WHO IS RESPONSIBLE?

On December 7, the Gila River sent a new flood into the Colorado, only 1,300 yards south of the newly sealed cut. At first, the flow into this new channel was slow, but it quickly opened until the whole Colorado River was once again flooding towards the Imperial Valley. Because of human intervention, the river was now attempting to open old channels into the Salton Sink rather than continuing south into the Gulf of California. Action had to be taken immediately or this new breach would become permanent.

The problem is that the Southern Pacific Railroad had already spent more than $2 million,[8] despite not having any ownership of the canal company that created the problem in the first place.

Twenty percent of the canal company's stock had been placed in escrow as security for the $250,000 loan made to the company, but the railroad had not foreclosed on the loan or taken ownership of the stock.

Who should pay for the cost of sealing this new breach? The cost was estimated at a staggering $350,000, and it was quickly determined that this was not a permanent solution to prevent flooding into the valley. It would take another $1.5 million to fully line a twenty-mile levee with rocks to keep the Colorado on its southern course. E. H. Harriman telegraphed President Theodore Roosevelt to explain that the railroad felt that it had gone above and beyond its duty. Since the US government owned most of the arable land in the area, including the Imperial Valley, it was the citizens of the United States who would lose out if the flood continued. More than 2,000 square miles of fertile farmland was once again at risk. He asked for financial help in making the additional repairs.

Roosevelt was sympathetic, but the land to be repaired was in Mexico. The United States government had no authority to act in a foreign country without its permission. And there were no funds to make repairs without action by Congress, which was not in session. The canal company, however, did have authority to act in Mexico by virtue of their Mexican subsidiary. Roosevelt argued that because the railroad had assumed active management of the project, even without ownership, they were now liable to act. He urged immediate action on the breach, with a promise to revisit how to pay for the full construction that was required to finally and forever secure the river in its current course.

Even though it made no financial sense, Harriman instructed his team to attack the new problem. First, they drove ninety-foot pilings into the riverbed. The pilings were washed out three times in the course of a month before they were finally able to get a trestle built. Once it was built, they started dropping rocks directly into the riverbed, since there was no time to build a brush mat. It was only after heroic efforts that the last breach was sealed on February 10, 1907.

Chief Engineer Cory reported that so great had been the demand on Southern Pacific's rolling stock and equipment that it brought nearly the entire railroad to a standstill, having required 1,000 flat cars and the locomotives needed to pull them.

Even in the midst of the crisis, however, the Southern Pacific civil engineers were very efficient in their use of resources. For example, a positive outcome of building railroad tracks parallel to the river to reach the trestle bridges across the gaps was that this new roadbed acted as a levee, with tracks on top of it to impede any new breaks along the line.

When all the costs were added up, the Southern Pacific spent $3 million to protect the Imperial Valley from floods. When the next Congress met, the President told the senators and representatives that in view of the fact that the Southern Pacific Railroad had saved land owned by the United States that would soon have a market value of up to $350 million dollars, and since they had acted in response to his presidential request, Congress should reimburse the railroad for the costs incurred *after* the December 7 flood. In time, a bill was introduced to provide $1.6 million. The bill languished in Congress and was eventually reduced to $700,000. This reduced amount was finally voted out of committee with a "do pass" recommendation after Roosevelt's successor, William Howard Taft, requested its passage on two separate occasions. But since the California delegation in Congress was small, a few Eastern senators said that this was nothing more than a raid on the public purse, and the bill never came to a vote. If left up to Congress, the Gulf of California would now extend up to Palm Springs, and the Imperial Valley would never have produced another piece of fruit.

Fortunately, the engineers and workers of the Southern Pacific created a permanent solution to the problem, avoiding the risk of future catastrophes in the Imperial Valley. It was a very costly solution that reverberates positively even today.

HARRIMAN'S LAST WORDS ON THE PROJECT

Towards the end of E. H. Harriman's life, a reporter asked him if he wished he had simply withdrawn from the project to cut his losses, as the railroad was never reimbursed and few people even seemed to appreciate the huge investment of time, money, and railroad resources. He replied, "No—this valley was worth saving, wasn't it?" When the reporter agreed, Harriman concluded, "Then we have the satisfaction of knowing that we saved it, haven't we?"

It was through the incompetence of others that the problem was created, but it was through the ingenuity and resources of the engineers of the Southern Pacific Railroad that it was resolved. Though economically unfair, it fell to private dollars to fix a public problem.

THE ALL-AMERICAN CANAL

In 1935, the Hoover Dam was completed upstream of Yuma, Arizona, and effectively ended the threat of flooding in the lower channel. As for the canal, it was replaced in 1942 by the "All-American Canal," which runs eighty miles to the Imperial Valley

A modern view of the All-American Canal.

Modern desilting works along the All-American Canal.

from the Laguna Dam near Yuma. With massive concrete head-gates, there is no risk of a new breach into the Salton Sink and the Imperial Valley. The canal's entire course is north of the Mexican border.

The All-American Canal solved many of the problems faced by earlier canal companies in that it includes a large facility to remove silt before it enters that canal. It has also been lined with concrete in many places to reduce seepage.

Today, the Imperial Valley has 650,000 acres under cultivation and receives approximately 1.5 million acre-feet of water per year.

The great promise of the early visionaries has been fulfilled, but only because of the willingness of E. H. Harriman and the Southern Pacific Railroad to save Southern California. Theirs was a sacrifice for the benefit of all Americans.

CHAPTER 4

1928: MULHOLLAND'S ST. FRANCIS DAM

THE HUMAN COST OF TRAGEDY

It was 12:50 A.M. near Castaic Junction, in the Santa Clara Valley north of Los Angeles.

"Charlotte Hanna and her husband, Kenneth, worked at the tourist cabins. As they stood outside, flashes from the direction of Saugus burst into the night sky, followed by a 'ball of fire' that lunged along the Southern Pacific railroad tracks. The couple expressed concern to seventeen-year-old George McIntyre and his father, A. C., an oil driller, who also witnessed the mysterious light show. A. C. thought it was static electricity from a storm. Convinced that something was terribly wrong and not willing to wait to find out, the Hannas ran for safety up a nearby hill. In the distance they could see headlights on Highway 99. 'I guess that's help coming,' Kenneth said.

"George McIntyre and his father became more concerned as they watched the mysterious lights and heard a distant roar. As George peered into the darkness, he saw something eerie. The tourist cabins were turning and moving toward him. Before he could make sense of what was happening, water slapped his legs and a powerful force lifted him away. A. C. McIntyre grabbed his son's hand just as [they were hurled] into the night. Terrified and helpless, the two were swirled along until they grabbed a passing utility pole. Water, mud, and debris pounded from all sides. For the older man it was too much. 'Oh my God! I'm hurt!' he shouted. He slipped from his son's hand and disappeared into the darkness."[1]

Façade of the Mulholland Dam in the Hollywood Hills.

OVERVIEW

High up in the Hollywood hills, due north of the iconic Capitol Records building, stands a beautiful row of white Grecian columns forming arches in what looks like a curved memorial. The graceful colonnade—decorated with busts of the California state animal, the California grizzly bear—sits atop a wooded hillside blended seamlessly into the surrounding landscape. The arches are in fact a decorative element on the crest of the Mulholland Dam, which impounds 2,800 acre-feet of water in the Hollywood Reservoir. Few visitors or residents realize that a large lake is perched directly above the homes and businesses of hundreds of thousands of people.

It's a little strange that the lake holds just 2,800 acre-feet of water, given that the dam was designed to impound three times that amount. It's also unusual for the face of a concrete gravity arch dam to be hidden by a hillside that fully obscures its 185-foot rise from the valley floor to the crest. It's as if someone wanted to make the dam invisible.

It wasn't always like that. For the first five years of its life, from 1924 to 1929, the gleaming stepped-arch face of the Mulholland Dam had stood proudly above the Hollywood neighborhood of Los Angeles. It was a dominating picture, showing America's increasing interest in large dams to provide water and electricity.

Then came 1928 and the St. Francis Dam, an identical twin to the Mulholland Dam, built in the San Francisquito Canyon northwest of Hollywood to hold water from the famed Owens River Aqueduct. It, too, was designed and built under the direction of William Mulholland, the larger-than-life chief engineer of the Los Angeles water system. But conditions in San Francisquito Canyon were far different than those in Hollywood.

WILLIAM MULHOLLAND AND THE OWENS RIVER AQUEDUCT

When William Mulholland arrived in Los Angeles in 1877 at age twenty-two, the population of Los Angeles County stood at 30,000. By the time of his death in 1935, it had reached 2.5 million. No one had a greater impact on making that possible than Bill Mulholland. He had started as a lowly ditch-tender, clearing weeds, but his natural genius for organization caused him to rise quickly through the ranks of the Los Angeles Bureau of Water Works and Supply, advancing to the all-powerful post of Superintendent and

William Mulholland.

Chief Engineer by 1902. In this role, it was his job to find water to meet the needs of the ever-expanding population and to build the infrastructure needed to get water to every house, factory, and building. He was relentless—some say ruthless—in fulfilling this objective.

Mulholland's most remarkable accomplishment was the construction of the Owens River Aqueduct: a gravity-fed system that carries water 233 miles from the Owens Valley on the eastern slopes of the Sierra Nevada Mountains to Los Angeles in the south. The original project included six storage reservoirs, 142 concrete tunnels, and twelve miles of steel siphons, through which water is drawn quickly down a shaft to pass under a valley that stands in the way of the route. Siphon action sucks the water up through a steel conduit on the other side of the valley and back into the aqueduct canal, where it continues to flow south to Los Angeles. At peak capacity, the original aqueduct delivered up to 300 million gallons of water per day. Its completion was an engineering masterpiece on the same scale as the building of the Panama Canal.

It also devastated the Owens Valley. To secure the necessary water rights to the runoff that previously filled the Owens River, Mulholland acted secretly on behalf of the city of Los Angeles, buying up land in the watershed without making his intentions public. This was a shrewd action, since landowners would have raised the price of their land if they had known the city of Los Angeles was interested. By the time local farmers and residents figured out what was happening, it was too late. Agriculture in the Owens Valley was deprived of water, and Lake Owens disappeared. The valley that had once been hailed as the "Switzerland of the Sierra Nevada" was left a desolate dust bowl. Towns in the valley suffered great economic hardship. Angry residents retaliated in the 1920s with the California water wars, in which saboteurs dynamited key components of the aqueduct and opened headgates to divert water from the canals. Despite their efforts, the Owen Valley economy collapsed, and many residents were forced to leave. William Mulholland won the war. And in doing so, he showed little sympathy for his detractors in the Owens Valley, saying at one point that "he half-regretted the demise of so many of the valley's orchard trees, because there were no longer enough live trees to hang all the troublemakers who lived there."[2]

Though despised by his enemies, Mulholland was a hero in Los Angeles. Some people thought he should run for mayor, given his popularity and name recognition. But he thought better:

"'I have tendencies that are absolutely autocratic and at times unreasonably domineering. It has always been a great pride with me that I have been able to secure and retain the loyal devotion of my coworkers, if not to myself personally, at least to the projects I have at hand. But I feel quite certain that in the discharge of the multifarious duties of Mayor I would utterly fail in this particular.' . . . 'I'd rather give birth to a porcupine backwards.'"[3]

Such was the temperament of William Mulholland. His arrogance and highly focused determination were great assets in serving Los Angeles. But this strong-willed overconfidence also led to a series of flawed decisions in the design and construction of the St. Francis Dam.

FATEFUL CHOICES

THE ST. FRANCIS DAM

Because Los Angeles is situated in a desert, with an average annual rainfall of just twelve to fifteen inches per year (compared to forty-four inches in New York City), it is perpetually on the edge of drought and disaster. Mulholland felt it was vital to store at least a year's supply of water in reservoirs close to the city. To accomplish this, he initiated an ambitious project of local dam-building to supplement the upstream storage in the Owens Valley.

Although designated Chief Engineer, Mulholland had no formal training in engineering. He was self-taught in all aspects of managing the water supply. This included his pioneering work in leading

The St. Francis Dam at full pool (with a visible leak).

the construction of numerous hydraulic-fill and rolled-earth gravity dams from 1920 to 1927. The earthen dams built for the City of Los Angeles were all successful. But the Calaveras Dam in Northern California, on which Mulholland acted as a consultant, suffered a partial collapse of the upstream face when the reservoir was filled with just fifty feet of water. The chief engineer for the city of San Francisco, Michael O'Shaughnessy, assigned responsibility for the failure to Mulholland-inspired design errors. He was not impressed with Mulholland's technical knowledge nor his temperament, writing that Mulholland and his compatriot F. C. Hermann were "so intensely conceited that they imagine all they might do should be immune from criticism."[4] Even though Mulholland was granted an honorary doctorate degree from the University of California at Berkeley, he was not invited back as a consulting engineer by the city of San Francisco.

In the early days of his career, Mulholland sought outside review of his engineering decisions. But by the time he decided to build the new concrete dam above Hollywood, he proceeded with no review or feedback, even though he had no experience in building a concrete dam. So confident was he in his abilities that he declared himself the primary authority on dam-building and the sole decision-maker on all aspects of construction. An impressive structure when built, the Mulholland Dam looked powerful and strong, and the reservoir filled with no problems.

Convinced that his design was sound, Mulholland next began engineering work on a similar dam in San Francisquito Canyon at the toe-end of the Owens Aqueduct. This reservoir would be filled with water from the aqueduct, to be stored for use in low-flow times of the year.

DESIGN CHANGES

Despite fierce objections from local farmers, who thought Mulholland and Los Angeles would use the dam to steal all their irrigation water, the St. Francis Dam was built, but not as originally planned. The maximum storage of the Hollywood Reservoir behind the Mulholland Dam was 7,900 acre-feet. The St. Francis Dam was expected to hold 30,000 acre-feet, even though it was almost identical in size to the Mulholland Dam. It seemed unlikely to many engineers that the new dam was heavy enough to hold back that large of a lake.

To make matters worse, the storage capacity of the St. Francis Dam was increased twice during construction; first by adding a wing dike on the western side of the dam to allow an extra 2,000 acre-feet. Then, during construction in 1925, Mulholland ordered the height to be raised another ten feet to bring the total storage capacity to 38,000 acre-feet.

Yet despite the fact that this reservoir was five times larger than the Hollywood Reservoir, no adjustments were made to the base of the dam to increase its weight or footprint. In fact, a comparison of the original design drawings and the final construction diagrams shows that the toe of the dam, which was to bite down into the foundation, was inexplicably *reduced* in size during construction.

All of this meant that the beautiful new St. Francis Dam would be highly stressed from the first moment the reservoir reached capacity.

FILLING THE RESERVOIR

Water from the Owens River Aqueduct was first diverted into the new reservoir on March 1, 1926. An astonishing amount of water was available, with the lake filling at the rate of 1.8 feet per day. Full capacity was achieved in May 1927, when the reservoir was just three feet below the spillways. At this point it looked as if the project was an unqualified success and the St. Francis Dam was hailed as the crown jewel in the massive Los Angeles water system. It was by far the largest in terms of water storage. Aside from the anger and lawsuits from Santa Clara River water users, Los Angeles residents took comfort in knowing that ample supplies of water were now backed up in reservoirs near the city.

But not everyone was celebratory. Some workers on the dam said that even though the dam was designed as an arch dam, no wings had been cut into the embankments on the east and west flanks of the main structure to anchor the arch. An arch requires a strong connection to the sides of the canyon walls so that as water presses against the upstream side of the arch, the load is transferred laterally to the abutments. With no notch in the hillsides to press against, the arch in the St. Francis Dam provided no additional strength. In other words, the St. Francis Dam was almost strictly a gravity concrete dam, solely reliant on its weight to resist the pressure of the water in the reservoir. That led to another criticism—that the dam was not heavy enough, both because of its inadequate size and because of the questionable techniques used in its construction.

For example, Mulholland chose to use local aggregate material in mixing the concrete used to build the dam. That choice gave the concrete a mass density of 140 pounds per cubic foot rather than 150 pounds, which was standard for the time. That meant that the St. Francis Dam was 7 percent lighter than similar dams with the same volume of concrete. The concrete also had a porosity of 13 percent, while the industry average was closer to 3–4 percent.[5] When water infiltrates concrete, it reduces its effective weight, which is a real problem for a gravity dam. Mulholland's field supervisors made it worse by using gravel straight from the bed of San Francisquito Creek without cleaning it. Worker Bailey Haskell said, "I could see these great chunks of clay going right into the dam."[6]

Criticism became particularly acute after the reservoir reached capacity. Multiple cracks appeared on the downstream face of the dam. The two largest cracks ran vertically from the top to the bottom in the center of the dam. Two additional lateral cracks also appeared on each flank of the dam, running diagonally from the middle of the east and west edges, angling up towards the crest. All four leaked, which alarmed many who passed by the dam.

But Mulholland assured everyone that there was nothing to worry about—these were simply "transverse contraction cracks" that were quite natural and caused by expansion of the concrete as it cured. Most dam builders at the time included expansion joints to accommodate the curing process, but Mulholland thought them unimportant. When the cracks started leaking, he simply instructed his crews to force oakum into the cracks to stop the seeping water and to then inject cement grout in front of the oakum to re-seal the face of the dam. While it is natural for dams to leak (all do), these four cracks seemed unusual in their size and orientation.

The reservoir had dropped in response to demand for water in the extremely dry summer and fall months of 1927. The dam had made it successfully through its first year and a half of operation. But when 1928 arrived and the reservoir started filling with January rains, springs of water began appearing at the base of the dam on the western abutment. The dam foundation was built on two very different types of rock, neither of which had much structural integrity. Pelona schist formed the base of the eastern and central parts of the dam. The western abutment rested on a Sespe formation of red sandstone. It was at the juncture of these two formations that most of the springs appeared. This meant that water was passing under the dam. Again, that is not unusual, since the immense weight of a reservoir creates incredible pressure at the base of a dam. Most dam designers plan for this in two ways: (1) they build a grout curtain deep into the foundation material on the upstream side of the dam to reduce seepage as much as possible; and (2) they install drains under the dam to allow a limited and harmless amount of water to pass through without damaging the integrity of the dam. But Mulholland chose not to install a grout curtain and only installed drains under the center section of the dam. The springs at the juncture of the schist and sandstone showed seepage outside the area provided with drains. This meant that the sides of the dam were being lifted by the water, while the center was not. That was the most likely cause of the large cracks.

When the reservoir again reached capacity in March 1928, all the leaks of the previous season reappeared on the face of the dam, with even more water issuing forth than before. The repairs of the previous year had failed.

Because all nineteen reservoirs in the Los Angeles system were now at full capacity, Mulholland ordered excess water in the aqueduct to be released directly into the San Francisquito Creek bed below the dam, rather than into the reservoir. This flow soon combined with water from the various leaks and springs bubbling up below the dam. This was the first time in two years that water had flowed down the creek bed and some downstream residents wondered aloud if something was wrong with the dam. Mulholland believed that it was nothing more than a happy surplus of water, something Los Angelinos had always wanted and now finally achieved. But to at least some of those living below the dam, something didn't seem right:

"By March 10, Chester Smith, who owned farm and ranchland in San Francisquito Canyon, had long thought conditions at the dam 'looked suspicious.' He questioned assistant dam keeper Jack Ely: 'Ely, what you sons of guns going to do here, going to flood us out down below?' Ely respected Bill Mulholland's leadership and expertise. His wife Margaret was good friends with the wife of Mulholland's son

Perry. Playing along with 'the gag,' Ely responded with a straight-faced reply: 'We expect this dam to break at any minute.'"[7]

Other residents half-joked to friends, "I guess I'll see you next week, if the dam doesn't break and kill us first."

Mulholland was annoyed at such talk, given his full and unreserved confidence in the project.

UNINTENDED CONSEQUENCES

MARCH 12, 1928—A CRESCENDO OF CONCERN

On the morning of March 12, 1928, chief dam keeper Tony Harnischfeger noticed a new leak from the west abutment of the dam. Because it was muddy with red sandstone, he alerted Mulholland, who immediately drove out to the dam with his assistant, Harvey Van Norman. They arrived by chauffeured car at 10:30 A.M. When they got closer to the leak, they judged that the water bubbling up was clear, although it had an odd pulsing flow. Mulholland concluded that the stream had become muddied only · after it flowed across some fill material on the west side abutment road. This allayed their fears that the dam was piping. In passing, they noted that there was also a small stream of clear water cascading down the eastern end of the dam where it abutted up against the Pelona schist, but judged it as no cause for concern.

By noon it was difficult to discern where all the leaks were, since waves caused by wind at the crest of the dam had splashed water over the front of the dam, wetting more than half of the downstream face. After two hours at the site, Mulholland and Van Norman assured Harnischfeger that there was nothing to worry about. They drove downstream to Powerhouse No. 2 to chat with the employees there. During that visit, Van Norman instructed the workers to open three of the St. Francis Dam's 6-by-6-foot outlet gates to allow water to flow down the face of the dam and into the San Francisquito Creek bed. He told them this was to draw down the reservoir enough to prevent water from being blown over the top of the dam by the wind.

A MISTY FOG

The rest of the day passed without incident. That evening, Lilian Curtis Eiler and her family were sleeping in their home near Powerhouse No. 2, downstream from the St. Francis Dam. At around midnight she awoke to a highly unusual dense fog or mist in the air. Having already worried about the safety of the dam, she immediately woke her husband, Lyman. He reacted with alarm, judging it to be a major problem. He thrust their three-year-old son, Danny, into her arms, pushed them through a window, and then went to retrieve their two daughters. Lilian scrambled up the hillside with Danny, afraid that something terrible had happened to the dam.

Farther up the canyon, a carpenter by the name of Ace Hopewell had passed by the dam at 11:50 P.M. on his way up the canyon road to his home near Powerhouse No. 1, which stood above the St. Francis reservoir. Although the dam was dark, nothing seemed amiss. But just before midnight, he stopped his motorcycle and side-car because he felt an unusual shaking in the road and a loud sound behind him. He left the motor running while he stopped to smoke a cigarette, then proceeded on his way. Little did Hopewell know that he was the last living person on earth to see the St. Francis Dam before its catastrophic failure just before midnight on March 12, 1928. The shaking he felt in the ground was likely caused when the first major section of the dam was blasted downstream by the force of 12.5 billion gallons of water pressing against the rapidly collapsing face of the dam. This triggered a landslide in the Pelona schist on the hillside and caused the roadway to buckle.

Mulholland's jewel had failed, and the dam collapsed in mere seconds. It was about to send a wall of muddy water more than 150 feet high down the San Francisquito Canyon on a path which would kill more than 450 people and destroy millions of dollars' worth of personal property and land.

VICTIMS AND
FIRST-RESPONDER HEROES

The dam failed at 11:57 P.M., as evidenced by the loss of power when transmission lines were cut by the massive wave. Within moments, a ten-story-high wall of water savaged its way down the canyon, smashing into Powerhouse No. 2 and the homes of its employees half a mile downstream. The leading edge of the wave arrived at 12:03 A.M. on March 13. The height of the wave (almost as high as the dam itself) shows that the dam failure was almost instantaneous, releasing the full leading edge of the reservoir into the canyon.

The first generalized warning of the flood to the outside world was issued by the crew at Powerhouse No. 1 above the lake. At approximately 12:30 A.M. on March 13, they dispatched a crew to find out what had disrupted the power and what had caused the tremor that Ace Hopewell had reported. When they arrived at the top of the reservoir, they saw only mudflats glistening in the moonlight. One of the men climbed a pole and tapped into a line to Powerhouse No. 1 to report that the lake was empty. Personnel there sounded warning sirens and notified authorities in Los Angeles. A dispatcher at the Bureau of Power and Light established a phone link with telephone operators in the towns soon to be inundated by the flood, who quickly passed the news onto emergency workers in those areas. This included sheriff's offices, Red Cross workers, and officials of the Southern Pacific Railroad, whose tracks crossed the Santa Clara River below the coming flood.

The first three people killed by the St. Francis Dam were the head dam keeper, Tony Harnischfeger, his wife, Leona Johnson, and their six-year-old son, Coder. The body of his wife was found upstream from their home on the canyon floor. This suggests that Tony and Leona had left their home and were making their way towards

A portion of railway destroyed by the dam failure in Castaic Junction.

the dam when it failed. A driver, who passed the dam shortly before Ace Hopewell, reported that he saw lights in the canyon around 11:30 P.M. This was less than half an hour before the failure and was likely a lantern used by Harnischfeger on his final journey. Tony and Coder's bodies were never found. It was Harnischfeger who had raised many alarms about leaks on the dam. Just that morning, Mulholland had assured him that all was well. Now he was dead.

The next to be killed were the workers at Powerhouse No. 2, downstream from the dam but still in San Francisquito Canyon. All were killed except for three people. Lilian Eiler and her son had crawled up the hillside with just moments to spare. They were found there by the only other survivor, Los Angeles Department of Water and Power employee Ray Rising, who lost his wife and daughters to the flood. Rising recounted the terrifying experience:

"We were all asleep in our wood-frame home in the small canyon just above the powerhouse. I heard a roaring like a cyclone. The water was so high we couldn't get out the front door. The house disintegrated. In the darkness I became tangled in an oak tree, fought clear and swam to the surface. I was wrapped with electrical wires and held by the only power pole in the canyon. I grabbed the roof of another house, jumping off when it floated to the hillside. I was stripped of clothing but scrambled up the razorback of a hillside. There was no moon and it was overcast with an eerie fog—very cold."[8]

Everyone else was killed, including Eiler's husband and daughters.

The next victims downstream were the Ruiz family, who owned a farm at the mouth of the canyon. All eight family members were killed as the floodwaters swept away every building on their ranch.

Once out of the canyon, the water caused havoc at Castaic Junction to the south, before turning west to follow the Santa Clara River as it sloped downward to the Pacific Ocean.

Chester Smith, the fellow who two days earlier had asked assistant dam keeper Jack Ely if they intended to "flood us out," was so unnerved by what he perceived as danger at the dam, he had decided to sleep in his barn with the doors open—on the night the dam burst:

"Sometime after midnight, the barking of the ranch dog woke him up. He could hear something coming, and the sound was terrifying. 'I could hear trees breaking and could hear . . . the wires on the electrical poles going,' he remembered. Smith had been in a flood before. Horrified, he realized what was coming. Without taking time to dress, Smith shouted to Hugh Nichols, his brother-in-law, and Nichols's wife, Mary, who were staying at the ranch. 'The dam is broke! The dam is broke!'

"Nichols had already heard a 'rattling noise, like one of those big trucks.' Now he 'couldn't hear nothing but just a roar.' The two men ran for the hills, pulling a frightened and hesitant Mrs. Nichols. The flood was close behind. After the three scrambled to safety above the waterline, they could see bursts of light from severed power lines, flashing like lightning. Exhausted, Smith looked down at the devastation. 'I never thought the water would come down like that,' he said later."[9]

It's likely that the homes at Powerhouse No. 2 were hit purely by water since they were first to be struck by the outflow, but that wasn't the case downstream. Each shattered house became a battering ram for the next target. Before long, the leading edge of the wave was clogged with debris, including trees torn from their roots, the wreckage of the concrete building at Powerhouse No. 2, the steel girders of bridges torn from their foundations, automobiles lifted from the roads and tumbled downstream, animal carcasses, and the bodies of the people who had been killed.

Perhaps the worst element of the flood was its timing. People were asleep and unaware of the pending danger. Fortunately, that was about to change.

PLACING THEIR LIVES AT RISK

Emergency responders sprang into action. Ventura County deputy sheriff Eddie Hearne was on duty at the jail when he received the news. He immediately drove his Cadillac *toward* the flood, sounding his horn and warning as many people as possible. He later reported that the speedometer on his late 1920s Cadillac reached the then-unheard-of speed of seventy-five miles per hour as he moved through unpopulated regions. He continued upriver, sounding the warning until his headlights reflected the water of the oncoming flood, which forced him to turn and head for higher ground.

Louise Gipe, a local telephone operator, called police departments to mobilize them into action. Gipe was soon joined by other operators, known as the "Hello Girls," who doggedly stayed at their stations, calling as many people as possible. The only information they had was that the flood was one hundred feet high when it exited San Francisquito Canyon and was heading downstream towards the Pacific Ocean. They had no way of knowing if they would be in the path of the flood when it reached their location in Santa Paula. Despite the danger, they continued to sound the warning, even while believing that they would likely be killed by the flood for doing so.

Police sirens aroused people from their sleep. One policeman became known as the "Paul Revere of the St. Francis Flood." After being awakened at home by the operator, officer Thornton Edwards urged his wife to take their son to higher ground. He then jumped on his personally owned motorcycle and started rushing towards the low-lying areas along the river. He made the very wise decision to go to every third house, pounding on the doors until the residents awoke. He shouted for them to get out of the way of the coming flood, but only after they warned their neighbors. He continued this pattern for as long as possible, even after the flood arrived. Edwards finally had to turn away when water from the flood stalled his motorcycle. He managed, with help, to get it out of the water and onto dry land, where he replaced the oil. To his relief, the motorcycle started. He then raced downstream, passing the flood, to join his wife and son. They were okay, but their home had been smashed by a long section of the Willard Bridge, which dragged their house nearly three hundred feet from its foundation.

As the flood made its way downstream at the speed of eighteen miles per hour, it sometimes widened to as much as 3,000 feet across and narrowed to as little as 400 feet. Damage was much greater in the narrow places.

As the flood came upon them, "Frank Thees quickly gathered his family into his car. His son, Frank Jr., six years old at the time, would never forget what happened next. 'I went into the water almost to my waist. . . . I looked back over my shoulder and saw the car, lights still on, with the water up to the headlights, . . . just two glowing circles in the dark. . . . Then the wall of water struck. I remember being tumbled over and ground into the gravel and my arm being pulled violently.' As the water rushed by, young Thees found himself pinned against a utility pole. Finally, he felt the ground beneath him. The flood had passed, and he was lying face down in the mud. As he struggled to get up, 'two white objects came into my view through the darkness. They were my parents coming out of the water.'"[10]

One of the greatest tragedies occurred at Edison Camp, a construction site on the Southern Pacific Railroad, where ninety-five men were killed as the flood washed through the tents of their camp. Some of the fifty men who survived did so because they had zipped the door to their tents. When the water hit the camp, the tents had trapped enough oxygen to float to the top of the current. After the flood passed, more than fifty of their cars were scattered like toys among the ruins of the camp. One of the men who died had a wristwatch, which stopped at exactly 1:24 A.M.—the time the flood had hit the camp. Of the fifty men who survived, nearly all had their clothing stripped away by the force of the flood.[11]

There were hundreds of other stories from that night of horror and heroism. Many were swept up by the flood but survived. Others lost family members: children were made orphans, parents lost their children, men and women lost their spouses.

It took a total of five hours and twenty-two minutes for the waters of the St. Francis reservoir to travel fifty-four miles from the broken dam site to the Pacific Ocean between Ventura and Oxnard, California. Along the way, it had caused massive damage to the towns along the Santa Clara River, including Castaic, Piru, Edison Camp, Fillmore, Barksdale, Santa Paula, and Saticoy. The record of destruction was staggering: more than 450 people killed; 909 homes destroyed; 1,200 homes damaged; ten bridges washed out; thousands of animals killed or injured; citrus orchards and farm crops smashed to pieces; and valuable topsoil scoured away in seconds. Electric power was knocked out over an extended area of Los Angeles by the destruction of transmission lines.[12] Yet, in the face of all this horror, heroes emerged to save hundreds of lives, both on the night of the disaster and in the days that followed.

With ten bridges destroyed, the survivors in the flood zone were effectively cut off from Los Angeles, the closest source of relief. The city of Los Angeles, working with the Red Cross and law enforcement, began to offer help. For example, the steel-truss bridge at Castaic Junction had been washed out by the flood, with wreckage found more than 300 feet downstream. Only the massive concrete towers survived, and crews went to work immediately to replace the destroyed section with a wooden trestle structure between the towers. It was completed in just one day. The land connection to the flood zone was restored, and relief began pouring in.

Because curiosity seekers and looters began to clog the roads, law enforcement officers had to establish a perimeter through which only people with official passes were permitted. Los Angeles City police chief James Davis sent hundreds of uniformed officers to join sheriffs in the affected areas.

The Red Cross in Santa Paula posted large signs throughout the flood zone that read:

NOTICE!

1. The Red Cross is in charge of immediate relief of homeless. Headquarters are at Old Mill Street School.
2. American Legion searching for bodies.
3. Morgue is at French's Mortuary.
4. Hospital is at Old Mill Street School.
5. Report all missing persons to the Red Cross Headquarters.
6. Relief supplies are asked for. Send to Red Cross Headquarters.
7. Chas. Millard is street superintendent.
8. Lee Sheppard, City Marshal, will sign all passes to devastated area.

The Red Cross provided aid to 2,490 people affected by the flood. The most immediate need was to find victims, both living and dead. For example, rescuers spied a baby atop a pile of debris. At first they thought the child was dead, but were shocked to find her breathing. No one ever discovered what had happened to her mother. Other victims were found half-buried in mud, struggling to free themselves. They were taken to makeshift hospitals to be bathed and cared for.

Fortunately, new technology played an important role in finding victims. With so many bridges damaged or destroyed, the fastest

"The Tombstone," the only surviving section of the St. Francis Dam.

way to survey the flood scene was by airplane. On the morning after the flood, no fewer than six aircraft winged their way over the fifty-four-mile flood path, flying as low as possible. When pilots spotted a body or a living person struggling, they dipped their wings to alert rescue workers on the ground to the location. Paramount Studios in Hollywood dispatched a high-resolution film crew to fly over the area, capturing images for newsreels that were played on movie screens all over the United States. "The valley looked wiped clean of every sign of life," the cameraman said later.

Victims were given temporary housing in relief camps, with food provided by the Red Cross. Within days, large fires were set to burn the debris piles and the carcasses of killed animals. This was a public health necessity to prevent the further spread of germs and pests.

In time, 450 bodies were recovered, or reported missing and never found. It's likely that others perished with no record, since many homeless would sleep under the bridges along the Santa Clara River. The high incidence of casualties made the St. Francis Dam collapse the second deadliest disaster in California history, surpassed only by the San Francisco earthquake and fires of 1906.

After the collapse, only one piece of the dam remained in its original position—a large unbroken block at the center of the dam. A local reporter with a macabre sense of humor named it "the Tombstone," marking the death of the once-mighty dam.

To its credit, the city of Los Angeles immediately accepted financial responsibility for the devastation caused by the flood. A joint committee was set up, comprised of representatives of both Los Angeles and Ventura County. Los Angeles issued bonds to create a restoration fund. While there is always some friction in such matters, these proceedings were remarkably harmonious, given the scale of the tragedy. A six-month statute of limitations was set on residents who wished to file claims against the relief fund for destruction of property and injury. It fell to the Joint Death and Injury Subcommittee to compensate victims' families for those who had died. Only a handful used the services of personal injury lawyers. All other victims accepted the offers of Los Angeles.

A FINAL FATALITY

The final human fatality of the St. Francis Dam occurred one year after the failure, when a young man fell to his death while scaling the Tombstone. His family sued the city of Los Angeles for creating an "attractive nuisance." Recognizing that the remaining blocks of the failed dam were a public safety hazard, dynamite was used to blow up the Tombstone and other large remnants. Today there is little evidence that the St. Francis Dam ever existed.

PROFESSIONAL HEROES—ACTING TO PREVENT FUTURE TRAGEDY

WHY THE DAM FAILED

Shortly after the alarm went out from Powerhouse No. 1, a telephone call was placed to the home of William Mulholland. His daughter Rose answered the phone, then quickly rushed to wake her father with the terrible news. As he staggered to the phone, Rose

The Hollywood Reservoir and Mulholland Dam.

heard him repeat over and over, "Please God, don't let people be killed." But people *had* been killed, and many of those who lost loved ones were angry at Mulholland. Within two hours of the collapse, and well before the flood had run its course into the Pacific, he was at the site of the dam, trying to understand what had happened. By early the next morning, he was at his office, under armed guard to protect him from the death threats he'd received. Mulholland offered to resign, but his resignation was not accepted by the city. Still, he and the entire project were quickly under intense scrutiny, with multiple investigations looking into the cause of the failure and its resultant loss of life, injuries, and destruction of property.

Three different investigations to determine the cause of the failure began sifting through construction diagrams and available reports of the days and hours leading up to the collapse. They made visits to the dam site and created a detailed map of the position of remaining fragments of the dam, trying to determine if there was criminal liability on the part of the designers and operators of the dam.

The analytical tools of the day made it difficult to deduce the sequence of the failure, which would be necessary to determine the cause. One group held that the west side of the dam had failed first, because the foundation was built on soft sandstone that had dissolved under the water. Another panel concluded that the east side had failed first, because of a landslide that had created a tidal wave that overwhelmed the dam's strength. Still other investigators thought the foundation and size of the dam was inadequate to safely contain the reservoir and that failure was inevitable because of the design, particularly since the arch was not properly supported on the wings.

Yet, when questioned, William Mulholland seemed to dismiss every criticism. He acted as if the dam was still intact and functioning. The district attorney, irritated, finally asked him why, if there was no danger, the St. Francis Dam had collapsed. When thus confronted, Mulholland replied quietly: "We overlooked something here . . . This inquiry is a very painful thing for me to have to attend, but it is the occasion of it that is painful. The only ones I envy about this thing are the ones who are dead."[13] Mulholland's misery was complete, but he still believed he'd built the dam with no error.

Despite Mulholland's unshakable belief that he had properly sited and built the dam, the investigations concluded that the likely cause of the failure was the result of building on very poor foundation material on both sides of the dam. This mistake was compounded by deficiencies in the design and construction of the dam. It was not built strongly enough for the size of the reservoir. Because drains had been placed only in the center section (which survived), the edges of the dam were subject to hydraulic uplift. In short, the dam failed because of gross incompetence.

Despite these findings, it was held that there was no criminal act or intent on the part of Mulholland or his department. The final Board of Inquiry recommended that no criminal action be taken by the district attorney. Mulholland was not going to jail. But the jury did recommend a significant change in future projects:

"A sound policy of public safety and business and engineering judgement demands that the construction and operation of a great dam should never been left to the sole judgment of one man, no matter how eminent, without check by independent expert authority."[14]

William Mulholland's career and reputation were destroyed. He retired in December 1928 and spent the rest of his life fretting about his fall from prominence.

MODERN ANALYSIS

Almost ninety years after the collapse of the St. Francis Dam, J. David Rogers was asked to do an engineering analysis using modern computer models to recreate the failure and to examine the various theories for the failure. Rogers's analysis suggests that the ancient landslide on the east side of the reservoir started moving as early as two days before the collapse, which increased pressure on the back side of the dam. His analysis pinpoints the exact spot where the dam first ruptured. It was a small block, identified as block 32, near the base of the dam. Because of extremely high pressure from the schist sliding into the reservoir, a section of the foundation gave way first, resulting in a blast of water shooting out and into the canyon, much like would be seen from the high-pressure nozzle of a firehose. It is likely that this high-pressure jet continued for up to thirty minutes, which accounts for the "fog and mist" described by the survivors at Powerhouse No. 2. This sustained release of water eroded the foundation under the east abutment of the dam, fracturing additional blocks that were then blasted out from the base of the dam. This scoured and eroded the entire east-side foundation. The concrete above the hole was now unsupported, with the full force of the lake pressing against it. The concrete in the east side collapsed into the breach, allowing a 200-foot wall of water to rush through the break. This further destabilized the Pelona schist, which led to an even larger slide into the reservoir. This second slide created a large wave that overwhelmed the west side of the dam. The dam had failed on both sides, leaving only the tombstone standing in the center.

Rogers's conclusions are the most plausible yet offered and are widely accepted today as the final explanation of what happened to the St. Francis Dam.

WAS THERE A WITNESS TO THE
COLLAPSE OF THE DAM?

It's necessary to use the word *theory* in describing all of this be-cause no surviving human witnessed the collapse of the dam. It's pos-sible, though, perhaps even probable, that chief dam keeper Tony Harnischfeger and his wife had heard the blowout of block 32 and were rushing towards the dam when the east-side base gave way, because Hopewell saw lights in the canyon as he drove by, and Harnischfeger was the only employee known to be in the area at the time.

If it is true that he was rushing towards the dam when it col-lapsed, he must have witnessed a truly awesome sight as the massive dam gave way just moments before the water killed him. Since he could not report on what he saw, we are left to draw conclusions based on the evidence left after the collapse.

AN EARTH-FILL DAM?

Paradoxically, a Mulholland earth-fill gravity dam might have worked at the St. Francis site. An earth-fill dam has a pyramid cross-section, with broad angles on both the upstream and down-stream slopes. That creates a very different set of loads than are exerted against a concrete dam, where the upstream face is flat. In a concrete dam, all the water forces are directed downstream against the dam. The thrust lines are always trying to push it forward. But the substan-tial volume of water that sits on top of the upstream slope of an earth-fill dam presses down on the dam, anchoring it more firmly to the base. A second benefit of an earth-fill dam in St. Francisquito Canyon would have been that the broad slope on both sides of the dam would have stabilized the schist field on the eastern side, rather than having the base of the mountain excavated away. There's no way to know if an earth-fill gravity dam would have succeeded, but it is telling that the Bouquet Dam, which was built to replace St. Francis in a nearby canyon, is an earth-fill dam that has lasted for more than eighty years.

Had William Mulholland stuck to what he knew best, the St. Francis reservoir might still be serving Los Angeles, and Mulholland would have lived out his life with acclaim. Instead, his last words to the coroner's inquest were: "Don't blame anyone else, you just fasten it on me. If there was an error in human judgment, I was the human, and I won't try to fasten it on anyone else."[15]

A New Risk Averted

As is often the case, there was good that came from this tragedy. The California legislature passed a new law that created the Division of Safety of Dams. This law required all owners of proposed new dams higher than fifty feet to pay the cost of an external review of their plans by certified civil engineers and geologists before they could proceed. This was the first such law passed anywhere in the world and has become the standard for other government entities since that time.

The positive effect of this law was immediately apparent. In 1929, a small landslide at the construction site of the new San Gabriel Forks Dam being built for the city of Los Angeles caused the new law to be invoked before construction could continue. Two independent panels of experts examined the dam site and concluded that it sat atop a huge ancient landslide. No amount of remediation could make the site safe for a reservoir. The dam was scheduled to rise more than twice as high as the St. Francis Dam and was expected to impound 240,000 acre-feet of water, more than six times as much water as the St. Francis reservoir. Even though a great deal of money had already been spent, the project was cancelled. One can only imagine the catastrophe that was avoided.

The Mulholland Dam and the Hollywood Reservoir

This chapter started with a glance at the Mulholland Dam and the Hollywood Reservoir. It posed several questions, such as why only 2,800 acre-feet of water are stored by a dam designed for three times that capacity. The answer is that after the failure of the St. Francis Dam, the residents of Hollywood were immediately concerned for their own safety, given that the Mulholland Dam was the pattern for St. Francis. William Mulholland immediately ordered the reservoir lowered, to take pressure off the dam while an analysis was completed. Although there were no apparent signs of problems, a panel of experts recommended that the maximum capacity be reduced as a safety precaution, mainly because Mulholland had failed to install seepage drains to provide uplift relief under two-thirds of the dam. Mulholland immediately complied, which likely saved this dam.

In 1931, more than two years after Mulholland retired, a second group of experts was empaneled. Their analysis suggested that the base width of the Mulholland Dam was insufficient to withstand any number of potential problems, including uplift forces, earthquake movement, or basal sliding. Rather than decommission the dam, the city began an expensive two-year retrofit of the dam that included placing 300,000 cubic yards of earth fill against the downstream face of the dam, to resist uplift and sliding and to provide stability in an earthquake. They also extended a concrete conduit down the canyon below the dam, to handle excess water coming through the spillways. Today, the dam holds back just 2,800 acre-feet of water, which is just 13 percent of the amount that the unreinforced St. Francis Dam was expected to withstand—a silent "testimony to the deficient design assumptions incorporated into the original structure,"[16] according to engineer J. David Rogers.

Today, the Hollywood Reservoir offers a serene scene in the middle of an urban landscape. Dams are crucial to our collective welfare. Because of the St. Francis Dam and the extensive regulation that followed its collapse, we are all safer with respect to the dams that serve us.

CHAPTER 5

1935: THE OVER-SEA RAILROAD

THE HUMAN COST OF TRAGEDY

"As daylight materialized over Camp 5, it revealed a scene of incomprehensible destruction. The few veterans left alive—eleven of the approximately 125 who had been in the camp when the storm began—saw that everything, every building had blown down. Gus Linawik remained up in a tree, his eyes full of sand, his ears burning from the blasting sand and the saltwater spray. At first, not knowing what was beneath him, he didn't want to climb down, but Blackey Lyons assured him that the ground was just below.

"'Let's go down and rest ourselves,' Lyons said, reassuring him, and so Linawik took a chance and felt around for the ground with his toes. Lyons got down, and so did another veteran. It was still raining hard, and Linawik was tired, cold, and hungry. 'My shirt was torn off by the wind and the back of my ears were sore from the waves,' he said. The three managed to find the railroad tracks, which had been picked up like a rope and tossed over the road in one place, out to sea in another. There wasn't much left of Camp 5, nor were there many left alive. The long bridge connecting the Upper and Lower Matecumbe Keys had fallen and washed away, cutting off their exit."[1]

OVERVIEW

One Atlantic hurricane generates two hundred times the equivalent energy of all electrical and fossil fuel consumed by all human-related activity in the world in its limited lifetime. Another way to understand a hurricane's strength is that it releases as much energy as 10,000 nuclear bombs during its lifespan of two or three weeks.

Neither of these comparisons begin to describe the awesome destructive force of the most powerful hurricane in history. It was on Labor Day in 1935 that hurricane-driven winds raged across the middle Florida Keys, topping more than two hundred miles per hour, the highest on record. The winds and ensuing storm surge flattened everything in their path. More than four hundred people were confirmed killed or were reported missing and never found. This toll included hundreds of World War I veterans who were building the new over-sea highway from the Florida mainland to the island of Key West, one hundred and twenty-eight miles to the south. Had the hurricane hit more populated areas, the death toll would have been even more catastrophic.

The human toll was paramount. But another unintended victim of the hurricane was one of the most ambitious engineering projects in American history: the Florida East Coast Railway Key West Extension. This "over-sea railway" was the improbable accomplishment of Henry Flagler, a founding partner—with John D. Rockefeller—of the Standard Oil Trust. The railway's completion in 1912 was hailed as an engineering feat equaled only by the building of the Panama Canal. But after the Labor Day Hurricane of 1935, the railroad lacked the financial capacity to repair it.

Henry Flagler was the last of the Gilded Age tycoons, the father of modern Florida, and the fellow who accomplished the impossible—a railway straight out into the Atlantic Ocean. The story of its creation is a great American tale. Its destruction ended an era of glamorous travel to Cuba. Well-heeled Americans traveled in luxury railcars to Key West, then transferred to well-appointed cruise ships to cross the Straits of Florida to Havana. Today, both the railroad across the sea and Henry Flagler are largely forgotten, though they both loomed large in an age gone by.

HENRY FLAGLER

Say the word *tycoon* and historic names like Henry Ford, Cornelius Vanderbilt, John Jacob Astor, and Andrew Carnegie come to mind. Today it might bring to mind Bill Gates, Steve Jobs, Jeff Bezos, Mark Zuckerberg, and other powerhouses of the information age. But in the late 1800s, the name Henry Flagler stood preeminent as a fully equal partner with John D. Rockefeller.

In inflation-adjusted dollars, Rockefeller still stands as the wealthiest American ever. Yet when asked if he was the one to come up with the crucial idea of incorporating Standard Oil and taking it public, Rockefeller quickly replied, "No, sir. I wish I'd had the brains to think of it. It was Henry M. Flagler." The key to their success was Flagler's insight that if they could control all the steps of the oil-refining process from extraction to distribution, with ruthless efficiency, they could bring their oil to market cheaper than their competitors and thereby drive them out of business. Flagler helped create the world's largest monopoly,

Henry Flagler.

and it gave him the riches he needed to lay the foundations for modern Florida.

Henry Morrison Flagler was born on January 2, 1830, in Hopewell, New York. His parents separated when he was eight years old. At age fourteen, he moved to Bellevue, Ohio, to live with his half-brother Dan Harkness. At twenty-three, Henry married Mary Harkness, a cousin to Dan Harkness (but not to Flagler). In time, he and Dan opened a distillery together, refining alcoholic spirits from grain. This led Flagler to an additional line of work as a very successful grain merchant. He was drafted into the Union army when the Civil War broke out, but legally hired a substitute to serve in his place. During this time, he profitably sold food and other goods to the army. He also sold wheat and wine in the Cleveland area through a commission agent named John D. Rockefeller. The two men became friends.

Flagler's restless nature eventually drove him to Saginaw, Michigan, where he thought he could profit from the salt industry by controlling both the mining and distribution aspects of the business. He invested $50,000 of his own savings and borrowed another $50,000 from a relative (for a total of approximately $2.5 million in 2019 inflation-adjusted dollars). But the venture failed when salt prices collapsed, and Flagler returned to Cleveland deeply in debt and humbled. He went back into the grain business to pay off his debt.

During this time, his friend Rockefeller had gone into the oil-refining business. His company refined crude oil for use in kerosene lamps and as lubricants for machinery. It was at this point that destiny stepped into their lives to form perhaps the most successful partnership in business history. Flagler happened to rent a home on the same street as Rockefeller and leased offices in the same building as Rockefeller's oil business. So the two started walking to work together and became even closer friends. Flagler was just thirty-six years old, Rockefeller twenty-seven. As their respect for each other grew, Rockefeller confided that he wanted to expand his operations.

He believed that he could eventually dominate the Cleveland oil market if he had enough capital. Fortuitously, Mary Flagler's cousin, Stephen Harkness, offered to invest $100,000 on the condition that Flagler be named a partner. The deal was accepted, and Flagler and Rockefeller were in business together (Flagler controlled Harkness's voting interest).

To meet the demands of competition, Flagler virtually created the modern corporation. First, he established exclusive rail contracts at deep discounts that gave Standard Oil a price advantage over competitors. It didn't take long for other refineries to fail financially, only to be bought out by Standard Oil at pennies on the dollar. Second, Flagler came up with the idea to incorporate as a stock corporation, which would allow Standard Oil to raise more capital from investors who held only a minority interest. He and Rockefeller would have full control of the business without having to provide all the financing. With no legal training, Henry Flagler wrote up articles of incorporation for the world's largest corporation on just two sheets of paper. Finally, because corporations at the time could only legally operate in one state, Flagler invented the Standard Oil Trust, which owned subsidiaries in each of the states where they did business—creating the first national corporation controlled out of New York City. In time, the trust held forty-one operating companies, and Standard Oil eventually controlled 90 percent of all oil production in the United States. Flagler was a true genius at finance and organization, while Rockefeller managed operations.

From Standard Oil's point of view, they were saviors of the oil industry, driving out weak competitors and enforcing price discipline that worked to the advantage of the consumers. For example, during the period of their consolidation, the price of kerosene dropped by 80 percent. But their methods were a source of great controversy. They created many enemies by making secret deals, threatening to bankrupt competitors who didn't agree to merge, and withholding shipments to strong-arm railroads during contract negotiations. In time, the Standard Oil Trust was subjected to multiple investigations and antitrust actions by the various states in which they did business. Their greatest enemy was Theodore Roosevelt, governor of New York, whom Flagler considered a scoundrel with no moral principle other than his own self-promotion. Though accused of crimes, no member of the Standard Oil board was ever found guilty of criminal wrongdoing. All these tribunals took a toll on Flagler, even though he was generally successful in fending off the accusations.

FLAGLER MOVES TO NEW YORK AND THEN FLORIDA

By 1877, Standard Oil was one of the largest firms traded on Wall Street. The decision was made to move the headquarters of Standard to New York City, to be closer to the financial markets. Flagler moved his wife and son to a fashionable home in Manhattan. He had little time to enjoy the New York social scene because his wife, Mary, had long suffered from chronic bronchitis, which eventually turned into tuberculosis. He was a devoted husband who spent his evenings caring for her. Even with the best of care, the New York City air aggravated her health, so her doctors suggested she might improve with a winter in the warm, humid air of Florida. At the time, Florida was a little-known rural state with limited infrastructure. Flagler accepted the doctor's advice and he and Mary made their way south to Jacksonville. The conditions were spartan, but Mary responded well to the environment. They returned to Jacksonville for several more winters until Mary Harkness Flagler passed away in 1881.

He was now a widower with an eleven-year-old son, Harry. Rather than raise the boy in the city, he purchased a magnificent estate on Long Island. He oversaw a complete remodel of the forty-two-room mansion, and built extensive beachfront facilities for the pleasure of his guests. This was new for Flagler, devoting his time to a pleasurable pursuit instead of business, and he was pleased with the results. His mansion became a popular place for entertaining.

Flagler found that he was as skilled at building facilities to entertain and accommodate people as he was in the oil business. This discovery launched the next phase of his life.

HENRY FLAGLER CREATES FLORIDA

Two years after Mary's death, Flagler fell in love with Ida Alice, one of the nurses who had cared for Mary. She was thirty-five years old and he was fifty-three. They married in June 1883, but business demands forced a postponement of their honeymoon. In December, Flagler proposed that they return to Jacksonville, Florida, to escape the New York winter. Once there, they decided to do some exploring in the area and wound up in the village of St. Augustine. This small town had the distinction of being the oldest continual European-established settlement in the United States. Both Henry and Ida Alice were taken in by its beauty and temperate climate.

But there were no hotels nearby worthy of their lifestyle. They stayed in the area through March, and then returned a year later. This time they stayed with an architect friend in the expensive vacation home he'd built in St. Augustine. Flagler was so pleased with the style of construction of his friend's home that he was inspired to duplicate it on a grand scale, so he and Ida Alice and their friends and family could enjoy the area in comfort. Flagler started quietly buying up orange groves at low prices and then announced to the world that he was going to build a 540-room, Mediterranean-style hotel: the Hotel Ponce de Leon. No expense would be spared in making it one of the great hotels of the world. There were many obstacles to overcome, but a year and half later, Flagler's magnificent new hotel opened to the public in St. Augustine. Newspapers throughout the country reported on the event, given Flagler's stature in the financial world. Wealthy families flocked to the Hotel Ponce de Leon to escape the cold. Flagler and Ida Alice occupied a suite in the hotel, and she started giving lavish parties for the socially connected who visited. Though the high cost of construction made it

The Hotel Ponce de Leon.

difficult to turn a profit, the hotel was fully booked right from the start and judged a great success.

The Hotel Ponce de Leon was lavish in its appointments, with every room fitted with electric lights and expensive furniture. Flagler was so pleased with the reception it received that he decided to build a second hotel, the Alcazar, to accommodate guests of more modest means.

When asked why he spent his time and money on a pursuit that could never equal the returns he received in the oil business, Flagler replied that he now desired to bring joy to people. It was an intriguing way to change his public image and to escape the acrimony of the various legal actions against Standard Oil. He remained on the board of the Standard Oil Trust and continued to collect handsome dividends from his ownership, but his focus moved south to his new home on the Florida coast.

Once he was in the hotel business, Flagler saw new opportunities for growth. His two hotels were at full occupancy, with potential guests being turned away. So he purchased the Ormond Beach Hotel, farther south on the Florida coastline, and renovated it to his high standards. But there was a problem—because Florida was relatively impoverished after the Civil War, there had been very little development. The few railroads systems that did exist used different gauges and made for a disorganized and impractical travel solution. Tourists wanting to go to Ormond Beach had to navigate their way on standard-gauge trains to Jacksonville, transfer to a boat on the St. Johns River, and then transfer to a different-gauge railroad for the final leg of the journey. This same problem existed for freight transport. The obvious solution was for Henry Flagler to go into the railroad business.

Flagler decided that such a chaotic system would not do, so he bought the railroads and built a bridge across the St. Johns. This was no easy task. Footings for the bridge had to be driven ninety feet deep to build a solid foundation, something that had never been done before. But this was exactly the sort of venture that inspired Flagler. With enough Standard Oil money available, the job was soon completed. Once the Ormond Beach Hotel was built out and fully occupied, Flagler started a series of railroad extensions down the coastline. So excited was the Florida legislature about all this building activity on the east coast, they started offering land grants to anyone who would build a railroad. As a result, Flagler was able to acquire nearly two million acres of land at almost no out-of-pocket cost. He was now positioned to build more than hotels—he could lay out entire cities to support his resorts.

Perhaps the greatest extension of his Florida empire began when Flagler traveled to the tiny hamlet of Palm Beach and declared it paradise on earth. He decided to make Palm Beach the jewel in his empire. Despite considerable engineering challenges, the rail line was extended to Palm Beach, where he built the magnificent 1,150-room Hotel Royal Poinciana, completed in 1894. Next was The Breakers, a hotel of incomparable style and grace which continues to welcome guests today.

With quick and luxurious travel available on Flagler's now-robust Florida East Coast Railway, guests from the north flocked to the south for their winter retreats. It was at The Breakers that the

The Royal Palm Hotel, Miami.

famed Palm Beach society season took hold, as many of the most prominent families in the United States made it their permanent vacation spot. This included many of those on the register of the "Four Hundred" that sat atop America's Gilded Age, a tradition that continues with prominent families to the present day.

The next stop for Flagler was a tiny settlement in the swamps of southern Florida with just fifty inhabitants. It was named "Miami." At first, he saw no reason to go that far south. Then an unseasonable freeze in 1894 negatively affected all his Florida properties but left the Miami area unfazed. Miami was warm when everywhere else was chilled. Thinking he could have a true year-round resort, Flagler was driven to build there. Getting a stable roadbed through the swamps was daunting, but in 1897 he completed a railroad extension to his new Royal Palm Hotel in Miami.

The citizens of the area were so grateful that he'd extended the East Coast Railway to their small town that they passed a resolution to rename the city "Flagler." But that was not Henry Flagler's style, and he urged them to continue to use the local Native American name of Miami.

Henry Flagler now owned eight of the world's greatest hotels. Married for the third time as a result of his second wife's mental illness, Flagler was, at age seventy-three, living an abundant and productive life. He was a hero in Florida. People were heard to joke that the abbreviation for Florida, "Fla.," actually referred to "Flagler."

However, while his hotels were almost always full, they were never very profitable, and the Florida East Coast Railway was considered to be doing well if it could simply cover its costs. Dividends from the Standard Oil companies had enabled him to build an empire, but his wealth didn't grow commensurate with that of Rockefeller because he kept spending his money rather than reinvesting his dividends in Standard Oil stock. It is estimated that Flagler poured more than $30 million into his Florida ventures. Now he could rest easy. Except for one last nagging ambition . . .

THE KEY WEST EXTENSION

What is difficult to imagine today is that the largest city in Florida in 1904 was not Miami, Jacksonville, or Tampa, but rather Key West, which had twenty thousand inhabitants. It was a propitious time for Key West because it enjoyed the closest proximity to the tropical playground of Havana, Cuba, a favorite destination of wealthy New Yorkers. Key West was also the natural guardian of the soon-to-be-built Panama Canal.

But Key West is an island, the last in a string of small island "keys" that form a curved line from the southern tip of Florida to Key West. The highest elevation of these islands is just eighteen feet above sea level. With no fresh water naturally available at any of the Keys, they were inhospitable places and largely uninhabited.

But their proximity to Cuba and Panama would make them an attractive destination for both vacationers and shippers if they were developed. Flagler envisioned the creation of a deep-water port in Key West that could interact with high-speed trains to the mainland that could profit from an expected bounty of goods and people passing through the Panama Canal. Plus, passenger trains linked to a Havana ferry across the Florida Straits would open vacation travel to

Havana even for people of modest means. Rail travel would shorten the transit time for all these ventures dramatically, compared to travel by ship.

It was a tempting proposition, but the engineering obstacles were more formidable than anything ever considered by rail builders anywhere in the world:

- The project would require multiple bridges and viaducts to span the gaps between the islands, the longest of which was seven miles.
- Building roadbeds through tough limestone and coral required entirely new construction techniques not yet developed.
- The bridges and viaducts could intensify the damage caused by frequent storms and occasional hurricanes through increasing the size and force of storm surges.
- Human-built structures could interfere with the natural exchange of ocean water between the Atlantic Ocean and the Gulf of Mexico, with unknown effects on sea life in the area.
- Uncountable clouds of mosquitoes posed a danger to the health and well-being of construction workers and tourists alike and would have to be eradicated.

Put it all together and it seemed a crazy and expensive proposition. In fact, when Flagler floated the idea publicly, it was quickly dubbed "Flagler's Folly." But he didn't care; public opinion often lacked vision. What did matter was the opinion of the engineers he trusted. It would be an arduous undertaking, very much like sending an army to war. Flagler hired talented engineers and completed feasibility studies. After examining all the facts, he asked Joseph Parrott, the general manager of the Florida East Coast Railway, "Joe, are you sure that railroad can be built?" When Parrott responded, "Yes, sir, I am sure," Flagler issued a simple command, "Very well, then. Go to Key West." This became the rallying cry for his workers over the next seven years: "Go to Key West!"

A 1905 company-generated article written to promote the project stated:

"As has been intimated, the assurance of the Panama Canal made the world look at the Keys of Florida and Key West from a new point of view. The canal opens, in a moment, tremendous vistas and pushes our commercial horizon across the seven seas. Key West is almost three hundred miles nearer the eastern terminus of the canal than any other of our Gulf ports. At the same time, it is the natural base for guarding and protecting the canal on the east and our great Gulf coast. That the island should be closer to the mainland has been the dream of generations. Now the dream has become a necessity to our commerce, our national interest, and our national safety. *But could the dream come true, could the necessity be met? The financiers considered the project and said, Unthinkable. The railway managers studied it and said, Impracticable. The engineers pondered the problems it presented and from all came the one verdict, Impossible. . . .*

"But strange as it may seem, there was a financier with the courage of Columbus, a railway manager with the administrative grip of a Menéndez, and an engineer as brave and as far-seeing as the pilots who brought the caravels of Spain through miles of unknown and uncharted seas."[2]

And so Flagler was compared to Christopher Columbus. The rhetoric was overheated, but the problems were real. Building a railroad across low-lying islands in oppressive heat among billions of mosquitoes made it difficult to recruit and retain workers. Fresh water had to be brought by railcar from Miami to the point where the newly laid tracks ended, and by boat to points farther south. Highly specialized equipment was required to build a roadbed in such conditions. Perhaps the most innovative inventions were two large shallow-draft excavators that would float in the shallow lagoons next to a key while dredging up limestone and coral and depositing it on the island to be placed as roadbed. Work camps and floating barracks housed the four thousand workers scattered up and down the Keys. These men had to be fed three meals per day, with virtually no local sources of food. It all had to be brought in by boat or train. It was a logistical nightmare.

The equipment required was considerable and included "three tugs; thirty gasoline launches; fourteen houseboats; eight

Laborers on the Key West railway extension.

work boats with derricks and concrete mixers; three floating pile-drivers; one floating machine shop; and more than a hundred barges and lighters. All floating equipment was fitted with dynamos to generate electric light, for the work was such that it could not be interrupted by nightfall. For work in shallow water, eight stern-wheel Mississippi River steamers were imported. Even these vessels, which could practically float on the dew, often ran aground. One disgusted skipper bellowed that the Keys had 'not quite enough water for swimming and too damned much for farming.' As for ocean going vessels, a fleet was required. Tramp ships carried crushed rock and coal from the mainland. Others brought cement from Germany, since all concrete used below high-tide line was of this imported high-grade mix."[3]

Though a hard and disciplined businessman, Flagler showed concern for his workers, setting up hospitals in Miami and Key West to care for workers who were injured or sick. He paid a fair wage for the day—increased because of the difficult working conditions that made it hard to keep men on the job. He forbade any alcohol at any of the work camps, although with Key West just ninety miles from Havana, it was easy for enterprising smugglers to overcome that problem.

Flagler's three key employees on the project were Joseph Parrott, general manager of the railroad; Joseph Meredith, chief engineer (who died before completion of the project); and William J. Krome, a young man who succeeded Meredith. It was up to these three to keep all elements of the project working and to adjust to surprises and delays. One of the most controversial decisions made was to keep working through the hurricane season, a decision that led to hundreds of deaths during the three major hurricanes that struck the Keys during construction in 1906, 1909, and 1910. Of these deaths, Joseph Meredith said quietly, "No man has any business connected with this work who can't stand grief." It was a hard time for tough people.

The engineering challenges were also daunting. The original plans called for building concrete ramparts across all open waters. This would make the railway virtually indestructible but would also block the natural tidal flow between the Atlantic and the Gulf of Florida (the part of the Gulf of Mexico right next to the Keys) on the western side of the islands. So, plans were redrawn to include bridges and arched viaducts. This added to the cost and increased the risk to the railroad in storms but was a necessary protection for the environment.

To give an idea of the scope of the project, consider the Long Key Viaduct, completed in 1907. This structure included 186 arches spanning more than two miles of open water. Rising to thirty-one feet above the surface, it became the highest point in the Florida Keys. The view from this elevated vantage point, when seen from an elegantly appointed passenger car crossing the viaduct, was spectacular.

The Gulf of Florida is a beautiful shade of turquoise close to shore, changing hues in fascinating patterns to that of deep cerulean blue farther out. Photos of the early trains crossing over the viaduct were so striking that they captured people's imagination all around the world, as shown in this woodcut that appeared in a Russian magazine. Flagler loved the image of the Long Key Viaduct so much that it became the logo for the Florida East Coast Railway. Constructed out of a special mix of marine concrete, the viaduct still stands today after more than 100 years. It is a testament to the quality of labor and materials Flagler insisted on using in his extension.

The most challenging accomplishment of the Key West Extension was the Seven Mile Bridge, which crossed from Marathon

The Long Key Viaduct.

to Bahia Honda Key. It utilized two distinct construction techniques. For much of the distance it consisted of heavy steel girders laid across massive concrete towers sunk up to twenty-eight feet below the seafloor. A swinging bridge allowed boats to move between the ocean and the gulf. The second technique was to build a viaduct of concrete arches like the Long Key Viaduct. When the Seven Mile Bridge was completed, it was nine miles in length because of the required approaches on each end. Crossing nine miles of bridge over open water truly was a rare experience for early passengers, given that the bridge itself was invisible beneath the windows of the railway's passenger cars. It appeared to the passengers that they were floating above the water with nothing to support them but air.

Despite the challenges and the enormous cost of the project, estimated at $27 million in 1912 (a remarkable $714 million in 2019 inflation-adjusted dollars), the Florida East Coast Railway Extension was successfully completed in January of that year. No longer called "Flagler's Folly," it was quickly dubbed "The Eighth Wonder of the World." The Florida East Coast Railway was now 522 miles in length from Jacksonville to Key West, 156 of those miles south of the mainland. It was with pride and joy that Flagler traveled on his own train from his home in Palm Beach to Key West. His arrival on January 21, 1912, was celebrated by more than ten thousand

Flagler arriving in Key West.

people, including the president of Cuba and representatives from dozens of Caribbean, Central American, and South American countries. A military band played patriotic tunes accompanied by a children's choir of more than a thousand voices. The mayor of Key West gave Flagler an effusive welcome and the people in the crowd gave him a ringing ovation.

It was a poignant moment. At age eighty-two, Flagler was in failing health. It had been his greatest desire to ride his own train to Key West, a challenge that had driven his work crews with unflagging devotion to make sure he didn't die before seeing his dream fulfilled. He received a gold-and-silver commemorative plaque with his likeness inscribed on it from the citizens of Key West. The men who had worked so hard for him the past seven years presented him with a golden tablet inscribed to "Uncle Henry." It was a fine tribute to an employer from men who had sacrificed so much to fulfill his ambitious dream.

As Flagler heard the band playing and the children singing, he leaned over to Joseph Parrott and whispered, "I can hear the children, but I can't see them." Then he said to the crowd: "We have been trying to anchor Key West to the mainland and anchor it we have done! I thank God that from the summit I can look back over the twenty-five or twenty-six years since I became interested in Florida with intense satisfaction at the results that have followed."[4]

Later, he turned again to Parrott and said, "Now I can die happy, my dream is fulfilled." He expanded on this thought in a letter to Parrott written six days later:

"The last few days have been full of happiness to me, made so by the expression of appreciation of the people for the work I have done in Florida. A large part of this happiness is due to the gift of the employees of the Florida East Coast Railway. . . . I beg you will express to them my most sincere thanks. I greatly regret that I cannot do it to each one in person. The work I have been doing for many years has been largely prompted by a desire to help my fellow-men, and I hope you will let every employee of the Company know that I thank him for the gift, the spirit that prompted it, and for the sentiment therein expressed."[5]

The cost of the Over-Sea Railway really was staggering. Consider that the cost of building the Central Pacific Railroad from Sacramento to Salt Lake City, 742 miles of track, including extensive tunnels and bridges through the Sierra-Nevada mountains, was $23 million. The cost of only 156 miles of the over-sea railway was greater! At this point in his life, Henry Flagler had invested more than $50 million in Florida. In his own words, "I would have been a rich man if it weren't for Florida."

Of course, he had much to show for his investments, including land, a railroad, and elegant hotels. His worth would have been far greater had he simply invested his money in stocks and other financial instruments, but his were tangible investments—places and experiences that gave people joy.

Despite the relatively low return of his Florida investments, his financial net worth at the time of his death would have been about $12.5 billion in 2019 inflation-adjusted dollars, a considerable legacy that would today put him thirty-ninth on the 2019 Forbes 400 list of the wealthiest people in America.[6]

Henry Flagler passed away at his home in Palm Beach on May 20, 1913, at age eighty-three.

THE OVER-SEA RAILWAY, 1912–1935

One of the great innovations of Flagler's railway was the use of large cargo ferries to move freight from Key West to Havana and vice versa. Three ships were put into service, each 360 feet in length, with docks built so that the train could back railcars directly onto standard-gauge rails inside the ferry, eliminating an entire loading-and-unloading cycle from the equation. Pineapples were one primary product being shipped from Havana, to the tune of 3,500 railcars per year. Cubans liked to cook with pork, so live hogs were shipped in the opposite direction. But after Flagler's death, the new operators of the railroad failed to build the large deep-water port facilities he had envisioned, so little of the Panama Canal traffic he had planned for made its way to Key West.

The "Havana Special" passenger service from New York was successful from the beginning. The trip from New York to Key West took thirty-seven hours and forty minutes by train, with an additional six-hour ocean cruise from Key West to Havana. Luxury Pullman sleeper cars made the journey simple for those who could afford it. Round-trip from Key West to Miami and back was twenty-five dollars, even less for permanent residents of the Keys.

Opening the Keys to tourists proved a boon to sports fishermen, who enjoyed staying in the small hotels on the Keys that were now easily accessible by rail. The extension allowed Flagler's adventuresome guests to enjoy a boutique experience quite different from his massive luxury hotels on the Florida coast.

Still, the railroad struggled to maintain profitability, particularly with the onset of the Great Depression in 1931. Many of Flagler's hopes for the extension were not realized, but it was an unforgettable experience for those who did travel across the ocean in the comfort of a well-appointed railcar. It was also safe. There wasn't a single instance of a train derailing on one of the many bridges.

FATEFUL CHOICES

LABOR DAY 1935

By 1935, the Florida East Coast Railway was operating in bankruptcy, one of the many casualties of the Great Depression. Postal contracts allowed it to continue operations to Key West, though with fewer trains than in its glory days. Nationwide, the automobile was already displacing railroads for local passenger travel and the idea of building a highway to Key West captured the imagination of New Deal planners in Washington. Politicians were always on the lookout for a public works project to provide employment to the one-third of US workers out of work. The Franklin D. Roosevelt administration supported the Federal Emergency Relief Administration (FERA) proposal for a new highway to Key West. Planning started immediately.

With unemployment running rampant, one would think it easy to attract workers, but the harsh climate and mosquitoes made it a challenge, just as it had been in 1905. There was a solution at hand—out-of-work World War I veterans who had moved into shantytowns near Washington, DC, urging Congress to advance their war bonus. The government refused. When the veterans demonstrated and became unruly, their strike in Washington, DC, was suppressed by General Douglas MacArthur, who ordered active army troops to fire on his World War I comrades. This had created a public relations scandal for the Hoover administration.

By 1935, the problem of the veterans had fallen to newly elected Franklin D. Roosevelt, who wanted to show more compassion. This resulted in FERA requesting that 600 veterans be sent to Florida to help build the roadway. Although not all veterans adapted to the grueling work and unforgiving climate, most did.

In August 1935, the veterans and other civilian workers were toiling away on the advancing highway. Thus it was that several thousand people on the Upper and Lower Matecumbe Keys, Long Key, and Key Largo found themselves unknowingly placed in the path of a historic storm brewing in the Atlantic. They were aware of the storm from reporting out of the Bahamas, but had no idea of its eventually intensity. Meteorologists also knew of the storm, but storm trackers noted that the highest wind speeds were only forty-six miles per hour when the storm was 150 miles off the coast. That was unpleasant, and likely to stop operations on the highway construction for a day or two, but nothing to be alarmed at. The barometer stood at 30 inches, which is considered normal. In other words, there was nothing to suggest anything more than an average tropical storm.

At least that's what conventional wisdom suggested. The problem with hurricanes is that they are wildly unpredictable. Even with modern satellite technology tracking a developing storm from outer space, hurricane-hunter aircraft that fly right into the center of the storm, as well as hundreds of weather buoys and other reporting stations, the margin of error for predicting the path of a hurricane is still more than 100 miles in 2019.

None of that technology was available to the Weather Bureau in 1935. The best they could rely on were reports from ships at sea and a handful of land-based reporting stations on islands in the Atlantic and Caribbean. That's why, even though disaster loomed, only a handful were alarmed.

It was this indifference that led to a significant loss of life, even though other signs pointed to a major storm. For example, Colonel Ed Sheeran, who was responsible for highway bridge construction, told Ray Sheldon, the man in charge of operations, that the island locals (nicknamed Conchs) were predicting a major hurricane. He told Sheldon that he ought to order the relief train that was supposedly on standby in Miami to start moving towards the Keys to evacuate the workers. Sheldon was in the middle of a poker game and quickly dismissed Sheeran's request out of hand. To send all 600 workers up to the mainland for nothing more than a tropical storm would cause unnecessary delays. Sheldon assured Sheeran that he was keeping an eye on both the track of the storm and the barometer and would act if conditions changed. Sheeran was unsettled but had no authority to order the train himself.

Just what is a hurricane—and what does a barometer have to do with gauging its strength? It is the difference in air pressure, measured by either millibars or "inches" in a barometer, that causes winds to stir. As hot air rises, it creates a vacuum at the surface, which draws surface air in to replace it and uplifts heat from the surface of the water. The warmer the water, the greater the energy of the storm. The winds begin circling counterclockwise because of the earth's rotation, which further increases the strength of the cycle. When the rotating wind hits thirty-nine miles per hour, the system is classified as a tropical storm; at seventy-four miles per hour it is classified as a hurricane. A low reading on a barometer indicates the potential strength of winds and, in areas close to the seashore, the likely height of a storm surge.

In view of this, Sheldon's assessment of the situation with the barometer sitting at thirty inches was reasonable. It was also deadly.

On the morning of Monday, September 2, the small storm exploded in ferocity to the east of the upper Keys. By 9:30 A.M., the winds on the leading edge had started to buffet Upper Matecumbe Key. William Johns, a reporter for the *Miami Herald*, liked to follow storms, hoping for a human-interest story, so he placed a call to Ray Sheldon:

"'I said, "Well, how is your weather?"' . . . 'He said, "It's raining and blowing like hell down here right now."'

"Johns asked Sheldon what he was going to do about evacuating the veterans in case the storm struck the Keys. 'I have two trains waiting in Miami that can get down here on about three or four hours' notice, and in case it gets too bad, why, we will send for them,' Sheldon told the reporter."[7]

This was Sheldon's second warning, but he was indifferent to the danger. Because of his lack of urgency, crews on the mainland had not worked up a train "ready to depart," let alone two.

VICTIMS AND
FIRST-RESPONDER HEROES

This was just the first of several delays that marooned hundreds of men on the Keys as the most powerful storm in history moved towards them:

- When Ray Sheldon finally did request the train on Monday afternoon at 2:00 P.M., it took two and a half hours to get the train staffed and moving.
- The train was then delayed by an open drawbridge that was allowing holiday pleasure boats to pass into the Miami River.
- In Homestead, Florida (the last stop on the mainland), the engineer decided to reverse the direction of the engine so he could back it down the Keys, believing it would be better to pull the train north than push it in the high winds. This took another hour.
- Finally, once at Camp 1 on Windley Key, a large telephone pole blew down, entangling wire across several of the passenger cars in such a way that the train couldn't move without derailing the cars, which took nearly an hour to disentangle.

The train that should have taken three hours to arrive did not make it to Islamorada on Upper Matecumbe Key until 8:20 P.M., six and a half hours after it was requested.

By then it was too late. The Labor Day Hurricane of 1935 smashed into the Upper and Lower Matecumbe Keys with a barometric reading of 26.35 inches (892 mb), which is the lowest recorded reading at the point of landfall in the history of the Western

An illustration of the train along the Over-Sea Railway during the Labor Day Hurricane.

Hemisphere. The Labor Day Hurricane also holds the record for the highest recorded sustained wind speeds at 185 miles per hour, with gusts exceeding 200 miles per hour. Sheldon was powerless as he watched the heavily reinforced Islamorada train station, where he'd been playing poker the day before while ignoring the advice to order a relief train, shear off its foundation at 8:00 P.M. It was destroyed, as were all the other buildings on the island. While struggling against the wind, he kept repeating, "This isn't my fault, this isn't my fault." Then, turning to an associate, he asked, "Do you think I'm to blame?"

The winds were at gale force as the relief train backed into the station. Sheldon and a compatriot struggled to make their way to the engine cab. At the beginning of their fifty-foot dash, there was no water underfoot. By the time they reached the locomotive, water had risen to their waists. The storm surge had arrived, adding the destructive power of the wind. Sheldon climbed up into the cab, asking if they thought the train could continue to back down to Lower Matecumbe Key to pick up workers from the camps there. Belatedly, Sheldon had realized the danger to the men in those camps. The engineer, J. J. Haycraft, said he thought it possible if he could keep the fire going, and he started to back the train. But within moments it lurched to a stop. The air brakes had locked, indicating a break in the high-pressure steam line between the locomotive and the passenger cars. Upon investigation, they learned that the swelling of the storm surge had toppled the baggage cars. Shortly after that, a second surge washed over the top of the locomotive's cab, extinguishing the draft to the oil burner. Now the men in the cab were in real peril as water lifted them up to the top of the cab.

"'The windows in the locomotive had been broken. It really was no protection except that you had your head up against the roof of the cab. I stood on the seat, holding onto a channel bar and a valve over my head . . . and there were times that we were unable to breathe due to the water breaking over the locomotive,' reported Ray Sheldon. According to engineer Haycraft, chaos raged around the men crowded in the locomotive's cab: 'The safest place we could find was the west corner of the cab, the only one that had unbroken windows. Gamble (the conductor) got in the corner, the Negro fireman, Will Walker, and I crowding around him. Bits of debris blew through the cab, but nothing hit us. The water rose to the top of the 'drivers,' the biggest engine wheels, that is about seven feet from the ground, and big waves came over us time after time, almost drowning us.'"[8]

The storm surge did not reach the land as a giant wave, but rather as the level of the ocean rising quickly. The Keys are too flat and low-lying to create splashing waves. The water simply swelled up until hydraulic action lifted the 150,000-pound railcars up and off the track, rolling all of them onto their sides. The steam locomotive, at nearly 400,000 pounds, withstood toppling, but was left without power. It's estimated that the surge was from eighteen to twenty feet. That was enough to complete the destruction of any buildings left standing by the wind. The path of the hurricane through the Matecumbes scoured a trail of desolation in which nothing was left, not even palm trees.

It's impossible for anyone who hasn't experienced a hurricane firsthand to fully appreciate the terror it creates. Consider that a seventy-five-mile-per-hour wind can drive a two-by-four piece of wood through a four-inch cinderblock wall. A 200-mile-per-hour wind isn't just 2.5 times more powerful than that, but twenty times as powerful, since the force quadruples with each doubling of the speed. In other words, no one else in America has ever lived through an experience like the World War I veterans and other construction workers in the 1935 hurricane.

Destruction along the railway.

That anyone lived is a miracle, given that many of the Florida Keys were completely overtopped by the storm surge. Those who were not in the direct path of the hurricane had to hold on for dear life or be swept out to sea in the Gulf of Florida. Some clung to the top of palm trees that somehow managed to hold their own against the wind. Others locked their fingers around the railroad tracks or sheltered in the gravel pits used in construction. While there are hundreds of stories recorded, here are a few that are indicative of the terror and suffering:

"Eight miles southwest of Snake Creek, Melton Jarrell is at Camp Five on the northeast end of Lower Matecumbe when the entire camp is demolished. Sixty veterans jump into trucks and head across the exposed fill toward Upper Matecumbe; they are never heard from again. As the water starts to rise, the remaining men try to make their way to Camp Three at the other end of the island 3½ miles away. When the water surges, some climb into trees or grab onto anything they can reach; others are washed out to sea. Jarrell recalled making it to the railroad embankment and hanging onto the track: 'A heavy sea came along and washed the track up and as it settled back down it pinioned my left leg under it. After lying there for what seemed countless ages, suffering horrible agony, I decided to try to cut my foot off, but I couldn't get to my penknife. After that I passed out.' When he regains consciousness, Jarrell is in a mangrove bush and rides out the rest of the storm frantically holding onto its branches. He is one of only twelve survivors of Camp Five."[9]

"A supervisor by the name of Frenchy Frecteau was sheltering in a hospital with fifty others, including some women and children. When the hospital started to shudder from the wind and rising storm surge he was swept away. Desperately swimming to get back to his family, he heard his wife call his name just as the hospital collapsed. His wife and two teenage daughters were killed when the building fell on them."[10]

Here is another survivor's account:

"Scientists still debate whether true tornadoes are spawned within the bands of the most powerful hurricanes. Bernard Russell can tell you that he has no such doubts. For a whirling vortex had snatched him and his sister and her baby off the ground as if they were twigs and was now spinning them about in an ever-expanding circle.

"Russell struggled, but he was up against a force stronger than the fiercest human intent. He felt his hands loosen at his sister's shoulders and saw the look of panic in her face as she was pulled away, still clutching her baby. Though he strained to reach her, his arms could barely move against the force of the cyclonic winds.

"As the vortex turned, she grew farther and farther away, until suddenly she and her baby were gone. In the next moment Russell found himself flying across the waterlogged packing-house grounds, just one more scrap of debris tossed by the indifferent storm.

"By the time the winds released him, and he could struggle to his feet, there was no trace of his sister or her child. 'It was like looking in a bottle of ink,' Russell was to tell *Miami Herald* reporter Nancy Klingener in a 1995 interview. 'You could see nothing. The winds are howling. And the rains are pounding. It was chaos. We were raked with trees or big pieces of houses or whatever else was coming by.'

"As he reeled about the wind-blasted darkness, searching for his sister and other members of his family, Russell felt his foot plunge into a tangled deadfall. In the next moment the heavy mass shifted in the wind, pinning his ankle, and Russell realized he was trapped. The winds were so strong by this point that he had to turn his back and cup his face in his hands in order to breathe.

"'It felt like eternity,' he says. 'It could have been thirty minutes. It could have been two hours. Time was nothing then.'"[11]

Yet another survivor recounted:

"Amidst the terror, the eye of the storm passed over the Matecumbes, leaving forty-five minutes of absolute calm and a star-filled sky. The terror of the winds was eerily silent. Then the trailing edge of the storm arrived, and the struggle began anew.

"John A. Conway was suddenly lying on his stomach with two other men, clinging to a telephone pole. 'Something just bounded off my back,' he said. He didn't know it then, but that something had crushed his spine in three places. When the water rushed over him, the others held his head above it and kept him from drowning."[12]

HEROIC EFFORTS

With both railway and roadway bridges washed out and telegraph lines down, it took time for officials north of the Keys to figure out the extent of the destruction in the islands. As news of the catastrophe reached Miami, relief efforts were organized. However, the main bridge at Snake Creek was washed away, so there was no immediate way for brave souls to venture farther south to bring medical supplies and food.

In one heroic effort, firefighters from Homestead, Florida, arrived at dusk at the washed-out Snake Creek bridge and set out in small boats to rescue survivors.

"One of the first they evacuated was Arnold B. Flow, who

floated across the creek at 11:30 P.M. Along with a couple of bruises and a puncture wound on his left leg, Flow had a six-inch-long stick driven below his shoulder blade and stuck against his spine. Ira Hatcher, [who had a] broken neck, went across at midnight, as did the injured Dr. Alexander. All told some 160 veterans made it across the creek Tuesday night. 'Every time we could get hold of an outboard motor and skiff,' said J. R. Combs, a Miami native who had helped build the camps the year before, 'we dragged it over and got across there.'"[13]

But that was on the northernmost Key. Farther south, it fell to the victims to help one another. Men who had hours before been struggling for their lives started rummaging through the rubble to find injured friends. There was little they could do other than apply tourniquets or strips of torn clothing to staunch the bleeding since the hospital had been destroyed and their ambulance washed out to sea. There were no medical supplies available. Still, they could cover injured men to warm them, move them to whatever makeshift shelters they could find, and give them company to end their terror. Some helped others despite their own suffering. De Forrest Rumage survived the storm with a broken back by clinging to a tree. As the winds calmed down to around forty miles per hour, he did what he could to help find victims. "'As long as I was on the go, it seemed that my back didn't bother me, but when I sat down that paralyzed me.'"[14]

Mrs. Carson Bradford, the wife of one of the marooned men, hired a private plane to fly down to the Matecumbe Keys to find her husband. On the first trip south, they could see nothing but a trail of destruction before being forced back by the lingering winds. But the next day they tried again and upon landing miraculously found that her husband had lived through the storm. On their return flight to Miami, they gave the fourth seat in their charter aircraft to a severely injured worker. This proved a good model for evacuating the most seriously injured. Soon a number of seaplanes flew south with doctors and medical supplies, evacuating the most severely injured survivors on the return flights.

Eventually, the US Coast Guard sent rescue ships and aircraft to the affected areas. But it was only after the governor of Florida flew south that the full resources of the government came to bear. One of his first acts on landing was to countermand the Veterans Administration's promise to bury all the bodies in veteran cemeteries on the mainland. Hundreds of corpses were simply not fit to be moved as the hot, humid air had caused them to start bloating. They had to be cremated to avoid a public health catastrophe.

Of the 695 World War I veterans working in the three camps affected by the hurricane, 259 perished in the storm, along with 164 civilians.

PROFESSIONAL HEROES—ACTING TO PREVENT FUTURE TRAGEDY

Ernest Hemingway, who experienced the southern edge of the hurricane from his home in Key West, was one of the first to sail north to offer relief. He was outraged by the failure of the federal government to evacuate the workers in a timely fashion, blaming it on indifference and prejudice against the veterans. He wrote a scathing article entitled, "Who Murdered the Vets? A First-Hand Report on the Florida Hurricane," published in the *New Masses* magazine on September 17, 1935, just two weeks after the hurricane. In the article, he accused the government of willful negligence.

Ray Sheldon survived the storm and maintained that he bore no responsibility for the deaths of the men under his direction. He believed that he had acted in good faith based on Weather Service reports. Public outrage was high, but multiple investigations concluded that the storm was an "act of God" and no one was ever held accountable. Officials in the Veterans Administration challenged these findings and suggested that a train should have been on standby in Homestead, rather than Miami, and that it should have been deployed much earlier. They also pointed to the fact that, prior to the hurricane, the veterans on the islands had been ordered *not* to leave for the north and many had been stopped at gunpoint from crossing bridges to escape. The FERA officials who had ordered this said it was done to maintain order and because they didn't want an interruption in the work. Some accused an officer at FERA of delaying the rescue train until it was too late because spending the $300 needed to send it south would have adversely affected his department's budget.

More than 400 people had perished in horrifying circumstances, with hundreds more seriously injured. It had been a largely preventable tragedy. Trains and trucks were available to evacuate everyone in the path of destruction and get them out of harm's way, but they were sent too late.

Fortunately, change would follow. Perhaps the greatest legacy of the hurricane was an increase in funding to better assess the risk of approaching storms, and to order earlier evacuations when there is uncertainty. The National Weather Service extended their network of ships at sea providing sea-level readings of air pressure and winds. They started using Pan Am Clipper aircraft to fly above the storms, providing crucial data on the pattern of clouds, looking for the telltale circling motions of a hurricane with an eye of calm in the center. And they opened more offices close to areas most often affected by tropical storms and hurricanes to provide ever-more accurate readings as a storm develops. With the advent of satellite photography and a broader network of reporting stations, today's weather forecasters can predict a storm path with far greater accuracy—although storms can still be fickle and make sudden changes in course. It is often just hours before a hurricane approaches landfall that the path the storm will follow is known, leaving nervous residents to wonder if they will be hit with the full force of the storm—or if it will veer northward while remaining out to sea. But today, weather models are accurate enough that people can be warned in advance to evacuate or make their way to safer locations.

A second consequence of this and subsequent storms has been continual evaluation and updating of building requirements to enhance safety for those who stay behind either by choice or necessity.

A third legacy of the 1935 hurricane has been better training for government leaders and others. Those in positions of responsibility are taught to take hurricane risks more seriously, and to react more quickly, so that people are not trapped through bureaucratic inertia. The worst aspect of the 1935 hurricane was that laborers who wanted to go north on their own were prevented at gunpoint from crossing the bridges. Essentially, they were made prisoners of that storm of previously unimagined ferocity. That is something that must never happen again.

FATE OF THE RAILWAY

The railroad viaducts and bridges survived with little damage, a testament to Flagler's high standards and rigorous attention to safety. But the same was not true of the roadbed and tracks. So fierce was the wind and waves that much of the track was swept out to sea or left in a pile of twisted steel and rubble.

With the Florida East Coast Railway in bankruptcy, there was simply no money to pay the estimated $1.5 million needed for repairs to the roadbed. The board of directors agreed to sell all their rights and property to the state of Florida for $640,000. At the time of this sale, the state appraised the value of the right-of-way, bridges, and viaducts at more than $27 million. Replacement cost was estimated at nearly $50 million. $640,000 was a paltry sum compared to the value of what the state received.

The railroad's death was not Henry Flagler's fault—he had built his bridges and track to the highest possible standards. It was the storm that precipitated the end of his grand vision, but the Great Depression and the subsequent rise of the US culture of the automobile were its ultimate killers.

All was not in vain. Flagler's bridges and roadway were put to good use. Rather than construct all-new bridges for the over-sea highway to Key West, the state simply built a roadway atop Flagler's viaducts and bridges. The beautiful Long Key Viaduct and the remarkable Seven Mile Bridge took on a new role: carrying gasoline-powered cars and trucks rather than steam-powered locomotives. The glory days of the Havana Special were over, but the practicality and flexibility of the highway was better suited to the needs of island residents. Henry Flagler had made one final, posthumous gift to the residents of Florida, and to anyone else who has driven along the Oversea Highway on US Route 1. Flagler's massive investment saved taxpayers millions of dollars.

Today, most of the original bridges have been replaced by new highway bridges that better handle the traffic. Large sections of the original viaducts and bridges remain, however, offering fishermen a perfect vantage point from which to cast their lines. The remaining sections of the railroad bridges were listed on the National Register of Historic Places in 1979.

CONCLUSION

The main boulevard in Miami is today named for Henry Flagler, as is Flagler College, which occupies the beautiful buildings of his first hotel, the Ponce de Leon. The Florida East Coast Railway continues operations as a freight hauler, and The Breakers in Palm Beach remains a premier five-star hotel. But Flagler himself is seldom listed among the great tycoons of the nineteenth century, perhaps from his reticence in speaking about himself. He once said in an interview that he preferred to let his actions speak for him, rather than his words. His actions were remarkable and bold—perhaps it is fitting that it took the ferocious winds of the world's most powerful hurricane to end his most costly and daring accomplishment, the incomparable over-sea railroad.

CHAPTER 6

1939: DEATH IN THE DESERT

THE HUMAN COST OF TRAGEDY

"Although it was still early, professional tennis player Tony Firpo had retired to his compartment bed on the left side of the sleeping car. Turning on his right side, he was dozing off. The rhythmic click of the wheels on the track seemed a bit faster than usual and he wasn't paying much attention to the speed of the streamliner. Nonetheless, the gentle rumble and swaying was soothing, and for him, it was the perfect way to fall asleep.

"Suddenly, he felt the sensation of very rapid, violent bumps. Startled, he opened his eyes and raised himself up on his elbow. Outside it was dark. But he noticed large sparks flying past the window and in those few seconds the bumps became more and more violent. As he felt the sensation of air brakes being applied, the car started to tilt. Immediately the lights in the corridor went out. His suitcases stacked neatly above his bed tumbled out of their lockers, striking him on the head and shoulders as he attempted to scramble up and out of bed. Then the car tipped completely over. In an instant, the car seemed to be floating through space. It landed with a tremendous crash in the Humboldt River bed, right side up. At that moment Firpo blacked out."[1]

OVERVIEW

A new word entered America's passenger-train vocabulary on January 31, 1935: *streamliner*. That's the day that the first diesel-electric streamliner started service from Salina to Kansas City, Kansas. It was a radically redesigned passenger train, with just three lightweight aluminum alloy cars that carried 116 passengers in luxury and comfort. It looked like a bullet, with a rounded nose and tail. Such a train was only possible because of a new high-speed, diesel-electric power-plant, which eliminated the soot, smoke, and chug of the steam locomotives. The train was named the "City of Salina" and it was the first of many high-speed "city trains" named for the most prominent city on their route.

When the "City of San Francisco" entered service, it was hailed as the most modern in the world, traveling from Chicago to San Francisco beginning June 14, 1936, over Union Pacific and Southern Pacific tracks. Here's what the Southern Pacific Railroad had to say about their new streamlined train:

"As modern as tomorrow, embodying spaciousness and refinements never available to passengers, the mighty streamliner, named after the metropolis at her western terminus, is truly a press agent's dream train. There's plenty to write about in bold exclamations.

THE **NEW** STREAMLINER "CITY OF SAN FRANCISCO"

SAN FRANCISCO - CHICAGO **39¾** HOURS!

TWICE as big • TWICE as powerful • TWICE as luxurious

SOUTHERN PACIFIC

Everything is the finest, the last word in distinctive passenger car design, ultra in the nicety of its appointments, sensational in minute attention to the smallest details. In fact, the whole train is colossal in conservative use of Hollywood parlance!"[2]

The transition from steam locomotive to diesel-electric was a thrilling new technology for passengers, given that the "City of San Francisco" achieved speeds of up to 110 miles per hour, with seventy-five mph the usual speed. Diesel engines substantially reduced the smoke blowing back from the locomotives, providing a better view and higher-quality air. Each of its three locomotives contained two 900-horsepower Electro-Motive Corporation diesel engines for a remarkable 5,400 horsepower combined. With this muscular power plant, the new streamliner boasted that the trip from Chicago to San Francisco was now just thirty-nine and a half hours—an astonishing reduction of nineteen hours from the fastest recorded time for the steam-driven trains it replaced.

To provide maximum comfort on the 2,100-mile journey, the train included air conditioning in all the passenger areas to keep travelers cool and comfortable while passing through the scorching Nevada desert. At a time when most trains consisted of just seven passenger cars, the "City of San Francisco" seemed to stretch forever with its three locomotives and seventeen passenger cars. It was a full quarter of a mile long, which meant that passengers in the rear of the train could watch the engines going in the opposite direction as the train wound its way through some of the mountain switchbacks of the Rockies and Sierra Nevada mountains. With a fully coordinated color scheme of tan and Union Pacific yellow, the train was made to look like one continual car from front to back that gracefully appeared to float along the horizon. The $2 million[3] "City of San Francisco" featured:

• Three dining cars: a thirty-two-seat coffee-shop kitchen car, a seventy-two-seat diner car appointed with table linens and fine china, and a luxurious buffet-lounge car where guests could enjoy

THE "DAYLIGHT" LIMITED
SOUTHERN PACIFIC'S NEW STREAMLINE TRAIN
OPERATING BETWEEN LOS ANGELES AND SAN FRANCISCO
S P
218

The Art Deco–inspired bar in a typical streamliner.

cocktails and snacks while comfortably seated on richly upholstered couches and high-back chairs. The waiters, cooks, and busboys of the dining service were tasked with serving more than 600 meals each day at an average cost of just ninety cents per passenger per day. The dining menu included entrees such as a "California Oyster Fry" of bacon, oysters, and eggs, cooked in a cream sauce and then fried like a pancake and served with julienned potatoes; "Filet of Sole As You Like It," fried with six oysters, six shrimp, and two fresh mushrooms sautéed in butter; "Baked Chicken Pie"; "Gelatine of Chicken"; "Mushrooms and Cream"; "Corn Fritters"; "Baked Filet of Beef"; and "Ham Smothered in Sweet Potatoes." These are just a handful of the mouth-watering entrees available on a train where all the food had to be loaded in advance of the journey, ready to be fried or baked to order, and then served by a white-jacketed waiter. For dessert you might order Caramel Custard or California Prune Fritters, Lemon Pie or Plum Pudding, Bavarian Cream or Old-Fashioned Strawberry Shortcake.[4] In all, there were eighteen desserts to choose from. It truly was an epicurean delight to dine on the "City of San Francisco" while watching the scenery pass by through the double-plated safety-glass windows.

- An eighty-four-foot, six-inch "observation lounge/buffet car" at the end of the train, which was billed as the longest luxury rail-car in the world. It included a fully stocked bar with a bartender to mix cocktails and other drinks to help the guests relax. This car provided magnificent views through large plate-glass windows as the train passed through the rugged landscape of the Sierra Nevada Mountains and the high-mountain deserts of Utah and Wyoming. It offered unparalleled views of the ascent through the Rocky Mountains, across Wyoming, and then on to the Great Plains.

- A fifty-four-seat "chair car," where passengers had assigned seating as they passed the day and slept in their reclining chair at night. These seats in the low-fare section of the train had far more legroom than any modern first-class airline seat and included bolsters for the feet while sitting upright and lower-leg supports when reclining.

- Eight fully appointed Pullman sleeper cars that offered a range of sleeping options based on the passenger's budget and preference. The open sleeper cars featured 168 berths with pull-down beds and drawn curtains at an additional cost of $15 for the journey, while the sixty private roomette cars cost an additional $22.50 over the base fare. The roomettes featured pull-down beds for sleeping that a porter made up in the morning while the guests were having breakfast. Then they could sit in comfortable lounge chairs in the privacy of their own room during daylight. If you became bored or desired company, you simply moved to the lounge cars for a game of cards or for a chat with other passengers.

- Passenger cars named after prominent sites or streets in San Francisco, including the Presidio, Market Street, Embarcadero, Mission Dolores, Twin Peaks, Chinatown, Fisherman's Wharf, Golden Gate Bridge, Seal Rocks, Union Square, Telegraph Hill, Portsmouth Square, and the most elegant of all, Nob Hill, the buffet-lounge car (SF-901), named for the most prominent neighborhood in San Francisco.[5]

- Public cars provided premium services, including a barber shop, shower-bath, and a stewardess-nurse who helped young mothers with their children, as well as any passengers who might become ill or injured. The train was even furnished with an internal phone system to call for room service.[6]

In 1939, passengers could still choose an older, slower train if they didn't want to pay a minimum extra premium of five dollars to travel on the Streamliner. That doesn't sound like much today, but this was at the height of the Great Depression, and five dollars then was equal to almost one hundred dollars today, so it was a special occasion to ride the "City of San Francisco."

CHICAGO, ILLINOIS—9:55 A.M., AUGUST 23, 1939

Men in suit jackets and ties and women in dresses and hats started boarding the "City of San Francisco" promptly at 9:55 A.M. on Wednesday, August 23, 1939. It was an unusually humid day in Chicago and the passengers were relieved to step up into the air-conditioned cars that would be their home for the next forty hours. Decorated in the modern Art Deco style, each of the cars had its own color scheme and patterns in the upholstery, carpets, and window blinds or curtains. Everything about the train was modern, from the electric overhead lights and side lamps to the extra headroom and width to provide maximum comfort.

At 10:02 A.M., Chief Engineer Ed Hecox pushed his foot on the deadman's pedal, which would automatically bring the train to a stop if it wasn't continuously pressed, and then released the throttle. The train jerked ever so slightly as the three locomotives began to ease their way slowly forward, taking slack out of the Janney Tightlock couplers that connected each of the twenty cars in the train. As the "City of San Francisco" made its way out of the covered terminal into the sunlight, people on the left side of the train pulled their blinds down to block out the morning sun as the train headed to the south, then turned west while finding its way through the maze of tracks and switches that made Chicago's the busiest railway

The "City of San Francisco" in the Oakland (CA) station, 1938.

yard in the world. More than 60 percent of all the trains in America passed through Chicago in 1939.

The "City of San Francisco" was a joint venture of the Chicago & North Western Railroad, the Union Pacific Railroad, and the Southern Pacific Railroad, since it had to pass over each of those railways' tracks on its 2,100-mile journey between Chicago and Oakland. As it streaked across the Illinois plains, the train soon achieved seventy-five miles per hour. Few automobiles of that era could go that fast, and then only on very short racetracks, since the roads of the day were of poor quality. For many passengers, this was the fastest they had ever traveled, and most hoped that the train would accelerate even faster. The twenty-four electric motors mounted between the driving wheels of the locomotives were continuously variable, meaning there were no gears or transmissions. This provided smooth and steady power right up to their maximum turning speed. On a journey that once took more than six months by wagon train, the thought of reaching the Pacific Ocean in just thirty-nine-and-a-half hours was truly remarkable.

Engineer Hecox was assisted on this particular trip by fireman Windy Kelly, who was also in the cab. On steam engines, it was the fireman's responsibility to keep the fire ignited under the boiler. On diesels, it was an obsolete position, and Kelly was really an assistant to Hecox in all operations of the train. Kelly and his staff went back and forth between the three locomotives to check on the diesel engines, the electric generators, and the large cooling fans that continuously blew air on the electric motors. They also maintained the separate diesel engines and generators in the "auxiliary power" car, which provided electricity to the passenger cars for lighting, cooking, and cooling. The train was a complex machine operating at the very cutting edge of technology, and it was an honor for Hecox and Kelly to have this assignment.

The journey proceeded without difficulty, sometimes passing through fierce rainstorms, but mostly through the hot summer air. Many of the guests retired to their sleeping berths or snuggled up in their reclining seats as the train crossed the border from Utah into Nevada on Thursday evening. They could judge the speed of the train by the interval between the chirps the steel wheels made as they passed over the juncture of one rail to another.

Some thought the train was going unusually fast as they made their way past Carlin, Nevada, particularly when a guest in the lounge car was thrown from her seat into the aisle, and two bottles of beer fell off an edged table while going around a curve in the track. The "City of San Francisco" was slightly behind schedule, but it was not unusual for the train to speed up to ninety miles per hour across the Nevada desert, even though that was above the posted limit. That's how they made up time in the schedule.

FATEFUL CHOICES

NEAR HARNEY, NEVADA—9:33 P.M., AUGUST 24, 1939

Around 9:30 P.M. on Thursday night, just a mile and half east of the small town of Harney, Nevada, the train slowed to sixty miles per hour, a necessary precaution dictated by the winding tracks following the Humboldt River midway between Elko and Battle Mountain. In a few moments they would pass through Bridge No. 4, an old steel through-truss bridge that had been refurbished recently. Engineer Hecox was at the controls peering out through the narrow windshield at the track illuminated by the train's powerful electric headlamps. Just shy of the bridge, Hecox noted a green tumbleweed lying against the rail. Tumbleweeds on the track were not unusual, but a green tumbleweed would usually still be attached to its roots, rather than blowing onto the track. It was just odd enough to catch his attention. Still, there was no reason for alarm—nor time to react even if it was a problem.

MALICIOUSLY INTENDED CONSEQUENCES

It turns out that the tumbleweed was placed intentionally to conceal a *huge* problem. The moment the lead locomotive wheels passed over the tumbleweed, Hecox felt the train lurch and jump the tracks. What just a moment earlier had been a smooth and effortless forward motion suddenly became jerky and stuttering as the steel train wheels tore up the wooden ties at sixty miles per hour. Miraculously, the momentum of the engine kept it on course long enough to pass through the columns and beams of Bridge No. 4. Reacting to the disaster, Hecox applied the brakes. But it was too late to save the now-doomed train. Here is how Don DeNevi described the scene in his book *Tragic Train*, which he wrote in collaboration with the Southern Pacific Railroad in 1977:

"The huge streamliner trembled, rocked, and swayed as steel snarled on rocks and ties. For a split second there was a terrifying rumble similar to a distant earthquake as speeding coaches furiously leaped from the rail. There followed a horrifying roar, as if a thousand freight trains were colliding. Resounding over the flat, quiet desert, the roar turned into the screeching, splintering, slashing sounds of crunching steel, as if some fiendish giant were squeezing

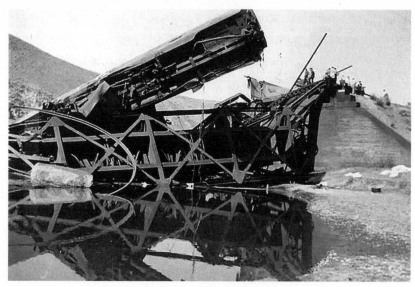

The wreck of the "City of San Francisco."

the train together in his mighty hands. Accompanying this sickening grinding of steel striking metal and rock, tracks being yanked from their ties, metal car walls made of the strongest steel being ripped open, folded, and crushed were the sounds of people trapped in terror. Death could not have chosen a better spot to strike. Out of control, the streamliner's middle coaches snapped their connections with the engines and slammed into the old iron bridge. Cars telescoped into each other, steel crashing and crunching. A dining coach filled with late dinner passengers and retiring waiters and cooks was tossed like a toy replica into the air and landed in a jagged, twisted heap in the river, with a club car nosing down after it; two other cars followed, hurtling against the heavy steel girders of the bridge, while other coaches simply overturned.

"The heavy, rusty steel girders of the bridge swayed, then snapped and collapsed like so much cheap tin into the stream below. Five more cars loaded with terrified, panic-stricken men and women toppled down on top of them. The beams of the bridge jutted in every possible angle, like so much matchwood. In the scrap pile of mashed hulls, the once beautiful City of San Francisco lay in the throes of agonized death."[7]

VICTIMS AND FIRST-RESPONDER HEROES

Once the locomotives came to a stop, Ed Hecox climbed down the ladder to the ground. His unit remained upright, the one following slightly tilted to its left side, and the third was almost fully laid on its side. Behind him all was silent for a few moments, then the desert air was rent with the sound of people shrieking in fear and crying out in pain. Recognizing that they needed help as fast as possible, Hecox turned away from the crash and started running toward the town of Harney to send calls for help. He ran without stopping for more than a mile and a half until he reached the small Southern Pacific depot. There he enlisted the help of the attendants in sending out urgent distress calls. He personally placed a call to Southern Pacific headquarters in San Francisco, telling them there had been a terrible derailment and asking them to send help immediately. Then he led four men back to the wreckage to help injured passengers.

Forty miles to the east in Elko, behind the derailment, Nevada doctors, nurses, and volunteer firefighters responded to the plea for help. Within ninety minutes, six doctors and twenty nurses were on board a special relief train that rushed them to the disaster site. A second train was formed in Reno, Nevada, more than 200 miles west of the crash site, which sent seven doctors and eight nurses, as well as Southern Pacific employees to help claw through the wreckage and rescue trapped and injured passengers. By 3:00 A.M. on Friday morning, four more relief trains were on their way from railyards in Ogden (Utah), Carlin, and Sparks (Nevada).

But at 9:35 P.M., none of that future help mattered. As the shock of the collision started to wear off, those caught up in the wreck tried to grasp what had happened and figure out what they could do. Many people had been killed, and many others had been

seriously injured. All power was out, which left the scene in darkness, particularly since the moon was obscured. Some of the cars
had landed in the river, and so a small group of men waded into
the water to rescue people. Others started building bonfires to provide light and warmth; the paradox of the high mountain deserts is
that they can be scorching hot during the day but extremely cold at
night.

Many people had been thrown from the cars through shattered
windows or openings in the walls where the long steel cars had broken apart. Perhaps the people in the most terrifying spot were those
who were crushed inside the wrecked cars, unable to extricate themselves from the crumpled steel and debris that had trapped them.

Fortunately, the last four cars in the train had come to a stop
while still standing upright. The two cars in front of those were
leaning, but not fully tipped over. The passengers in these cars had
experienced trauma from being thrown forward as the train came
to such an abrupt halt, but many were able to exit their cars. They
moved forward to aid the passengers in the five cars that had been
demolished by the crash into the bridge.

For example, as professional tennis player Tony Firpo regained
consciousness, he found himself bleeding from a variety of cuts
and wounds. He was surrounded by broken glass. In a matter of
moments, other passengers assembled near his room and suggested
that they break the glass in the window to escape before the railcar
caught fire. Firpo tore a piece of metal from a bar table and used it
to shatter the window. He crawled on top of the wrecked train car
and started lifting passengers from inside the car and then helped
them get down the side onto the riverbank. After helping eight
people, he moved to other cars to repeat the procedure. Although
he was in great pain from his cuts, he continued to help injured
people as best he could. Finally, at 4:00 A.M., he boarded a relief
train headed to the Elko hospital.

There were hundreds of heroic deeds performed that night,
many by passengers and crew members who were themselves

injured. Four stories illustrate how passengers and crew helped one another:

Ernest Betts was traveling from Pennsylvania. He had been thrown clear of the train with such force that it tore his shoes off. Wandering barefoot in the darkness, he found a man bleeding profusely. Acting on instinct, and with nothing more than a basic knowledge of first aid, he tore some of his own clothing into bandages and applied a tourniquet above the man's wound, saving his life. Soon Ernest was tearing more clothing into bandages and binding up wounds on dozens more wounded. He'd tell his fellow passengers that it was going to "hurt like hell," but that they should hang on. His voice had a calming effect on people, and many thanked him for his actions and steady resolve.

One of those who thanked Betts was the only doctor on the train, Dr. F. G. Brigham. Brigham had fallen asleep early that night. He was on his way to California for a much-needed vacation. He awoke to find himself in water up to the level of his sleeping berth when the train crashed. He had to fight his way out of a mostly submerged compartment by smashing a window and climbing out past the body of the porter who had helped him earlier that evening. Once out of his cabin, he used a small flashlight he'd brought along to smash through cabin windows in other wrecked cars. He administered relief to dozens of injured passengers, using bandages and morphine from a small emergency kit to ease their pain. Dr. Brigham said that Ernest Betts "'was the real Samaritan in the wilderness who all by himself saved the ebbing lives of at least [thirty] passengers. Probably more! He simply wouldn't let them die. Although not a medical doctor and although his system of hand bandages and tourniquets were crude as the niceties of medical practice go, he stopped the flow of blood long before dawn until I could get there. Some of his bandages I changed only to prevent gangrene from setting in.'

"The doctor saved dozens of people as he applied expert medical care in these extreme circumstances. In a modest gesture he gave credit to the battered flashlight he carried in his coat pocket, saying,

'This saved a lot of lives.'"[8] Going into more detail he recorded, "I treated everyone I could in my car and then climbed out to help with the survivors who had been removed. It was the most horrible sight I ever saw—and remember that I was with the Medical Corps in the World War. They were horribly mutilated. I saw fractures where the broken limbs could be turned completely around."[9]

Edgar Metoyer was an African-American porter on the train who waded into the river time and again to carry people to safety. On one occasion, he dove into the muddy river to drag a survivor back up to the air and into life. He was aided for part of the night by Tony Sherman, a bartender, who helped Metoyer rescue many people before collapsing from the trauma of his own broken ribs. After making sure everyone, living and dead, had been pulled from the river, Metoyer spent the rest of the night going back into the cars for blankets and mattresses and getting whiskey for patients at the request of the doctors.

Dr. Brigham saved his highest praise for an unknown porter who refused his help, insisting that Brigham attend to the passengers first. "'I don't even know his name,' Dr. Brigham told reporters the next day in San Francisco. 'His was one of the worst torn bodies in the wreck. The porter's left foot was slashed away at the ankle. His upper leg was broken so bad that the thigh bone protruded from the wound. His shoulder also was crushed and broken. I have never seen such a case of self-denial. "Don't bother with me, Doc. Tend to the passengers first," he implored. 'That was heroism one doesn't meet in my profession or any other very often. I stopped the flow of blood from his ankle and I gave him first aid before he made me move on. That man's smile carried me through what was an awful night.'"[10] By the time he boarded a relief train the next morning to continue his journey on to California, he was thoroughly exhausted.

In time, rescuers from the nearby towns and the special rescue trains started arriving. As the doctors from Elko and then Reno arrived, they were able to provide the high-quality emergency care needed by the survivors. They immediately went to work searching through the rubble to find people trapped by the twisted steel. Once found, passengers were carried to a makeshift hospital on the desert floor that was close to the warmth of the bonfires. One passenger recorded that she had never been so happy as when a local cowboy worked to clear her from the wreckage that trapped her and then carried her to safety.

When the sun rose on the scene the following morning, hundreds of rescuers had arrived. They helped some of the survivors onto rescue trains that would take them to hospitals and the advanced medical care they needed. Some of the survivors with only minor injuries found their way onto trains heading to California and quickly disappeared into their own lives.

As the Southern Pacific raced to send rescue and salvage crews, they were fortunate to have use of the tracks of the Western Pacific Railroad, which ran parallel to the Southern Pacific lines at this spot. With the bridge destroyed, it would be several months before the Southern Pacific tracks could be cleared and restored.

When the final count was taken, twenty-four people had lost their lives and 121 had been injured.

PROFESSIONAL HEROES—ACTING TO PREVENT FUTURE TRAGEDY

SABOTAGE OR NEGLIGENCE?

It was easy for investigators to find the spot where the train derailed because of the torn-up railroad ties. What they found was evidence of sabotage. They quickly asserted that this was not an accident—it was murder and intentional destruction of property. The primary evidence for this charge was that the spikes that held the rail on the south side of the tracks had been pried loose from the wooden ties, the rail moved four inches closer to the northern rail, and then re-spiked just enough to hold the rail in place. Additionally, the end-face of the moved rail had been painted with brown paint to keep it from reflecting the oncoming streamliner's headlamp when it came around the corner. Finally, the bond wires that sent an electrical signal along the rails had been stretched to keep the moved rail in contact with the leading rail, so the engineer would have no warning that there was a break in the line.

Moving a rail four inches to the left meant that the train was destined to derail. Because a slow-moving freight train had passed over the same spot four hours earlier without incident, it was clear that the "City of San Francisco" was the intended target of this sabotage and that it had taken place after the earlier train had passed.

Why would someone commit such a horrible act? The Southern Pacific indicated that there were three possible motives: (1) to gain revenge against the railroad for some grievance—it was usually an employee who sought this kind of injury; (2) to loot the train, stealing mail or passengers' valuables after the train was wrecked; or (3) to commit an impulsive, criminally insane act.

In other words, this wasn't the first time that someone had attempted to derail a train. It was just the worst instance in Southern Pacific history.

Not everyone believed that sabotage was the real cause of the disaster. Several newspapers in the area speculated that the "City of San Francisco" was simply going too fast to negotiate the track because the engineer wanted to make up lost time in the schedule for an on-time arrival in Oakland. After all, he had remarked earlier that night that they could go ninety miles per hour through Nevada to make up time. Several of the surviving passengers thought that the train was going much faster than the posted speed of sixty miles per hour at the time of the crash. The only proof to be had that the train had been going the posted speed was Ed Hecox's personal word—and he had obvious motive for that claim if speed was in fact the reason for the derailment. In this theory, the motive for declaring the derailment the result of sabotage was to deflect blame from railroad malfeasance to unknown saboteurs. To support this claim, some of the locals who had arrived on the scene that morning alleged that they had witnessed Southern Pacific employees moving the track after the crash to make it appear that sabotage was the cause rather than negligence on the part of the railroad.

The resolution of these conflicting claims was of great financial importance to the railroad. If the disaster was caused by external malice, their liability to passengers was greatly reduced. If the crash was a result of negligence, they faced far higher civil penalties and settlement costs.

Chief Special Agent Dan O'Connell was immediately dispatched from Southern Pacific headquarters in San Francisco to investigate the cause of the derailment. But by the time he arrived on Friday, thousands had tramped through the area during the rescue efforts, contaminating the crash scene. Fortunately, some of the early-arriving Southern Pacific personnel had taken photos of the moved track with its fresh coat of brown paint. O'Connell ordered many additional photos taken to keep the record as accurate as possible. He concluded that if this had been done within the four-hour window after the earlier passage of the freight train, there must be evidence in the vicinity of the tools used to cause the derailment.

The first clue to support sabotage was that one of the maintenance crews in the area had reported earlier that a toolbox had been stolen with the right kind of equipment to move a rail. O'Connell studied the terrain and maps of the area, working on the theory that the saboteurs were interested in robbing the train. He concluded that if they needed to stay within viewing distance of the accident to know when to plunder the stricken site but still be able to leave the scene quickly, they most likely would have discarded their heavy tools in the river to keep them from being found. He hired four local divers to scour the deepest pools downstream from the wreckage. These young men—Grant Stevenson, Dennis Willmore, Jesse Walker, and Fred Gasaway—began a methodical search of the cold river. O'Connell told them to work quickly, but not under pressure. He was prepared to continue the search for months if necessary. Fortunately, the divers found a tool that first afternoon, after only nine hours of diving. Three divers were needed to pull a heavy jack, capable of moving twenty-five tons of steel, from the river. If sabotage was the cause, the jack would have been a necessary tool to lift the heavy steel rail. Although it took weeks to find all the tools involved, one by one, heavy steel wrenches and crowbars were extracted from the river. The biggest break of all came when one of the young divers found a tool wrapped in a blue jacket deep under the water. A tan jacket was also found some distance away. Now the detectives had clues as to the size of the men who were likely involved, as well as visual clues they could use in posting a $10,000 reward for information leading to the arrest and conviction of the perpetrators.

O'Connell became obsessed with this project. Once the jackets had been extracted, he initiated a nationwide search to find where the jackets had been made and sold. This required his detectives to contact hundreds of clothing manufacturers. Eventually, they found the sources for both jackets. With respect to the blue jacket, the manufacturer said that 12,000 of that jacket had been made. O'Connell decided to trace all of them to find the man responsible, since soaking in the river might have altered the size. After contacting more than 1,000 stores, they found a paint store in Ogden, Utah, where a young clerk said that she had seen a man wearing that jacket buying brown paint. She recognized the jacket because the back had been torn in an unusual way and there was an odd stitching pattern that had been used to patch another tear in the fabric. Her story was verified by another clerk, who had seen the man in the blue jacket as well as another man wearing a tan jacket. Perhaps these were the two saboteurs. Unfortunately, nearly all transactions in 1939 were in cash, so no one had written down the names of the two customers. The young ladies were unable to provide a good description of the men. Ogden was the closest major city to the crash site, so it was credible that the men had passed through that way.

Concurrent with the efforts to trace the tools and the two jackets worn by the saboteurs, O'Connell and local police departments, in cooperation with the FBI, interviewed hundreds of out-of-work men who were known to have been in the area on the night of the accident. Whenever they seemed to find a likely candidate, the person either had an alibi or could not be placed at the scene of the crime. One young man confessed to the crime, but when O'Connell flew him to the scene of the crash, he could not provide essential details that the saboteur most certainly would have known. His confession was determined to be false.

O'Connell and his team spared no effort in their determination to find the culprits. By the end of February 1940, he and his detectives had investigated 362 clues and interviewed hundreds of railroad employees, residents of nearby towns, area mental patients, and former railroad employees. They also joined in 533 interviews suggested by the FBI. The total number of people interviewed from August to February totaled 93,110. Despite the substantial reward to attract clues and all the FBI's other efforts, the guilty parties were never found.

While public interest had been extremely high immediately after the derailment, the invasion of Poland by Nazi Germany in September 1939 moved the story off the front pages of the newspapers, and the trail grew cold. Still O'Connell persisted. He and his team interviewed trespassers and other indigents, as well as criminals suggested by local authorities. By the time he retired in 1944, Agent O'Connell had personally interviewed 12,579 individuals and his team had questioned an additional 197,858. It was one of the largest manhunts in history, but it ended with no arrests or convictions.[11]

While the perpetrator was never found, the relentless investigation by the Southern Pacific over more than a decade, as well as the continued offering of a substantial reward, had the effect of increasing railroad security and keeping other possible sabotage at bay. Only one other incident of this type has occurred since 1939, and that was against an Amtrak train in 1995 in southern Arizona, almost six decades later.

In March 1941, Eleanor and Harry Wallor filed a lawsuit in San Francisco seeking compensation for their injuries as a result of negligence on the part of the Southern Pacific Railroad. They first alleged that sabotage was not the cause of the accident, asserting that all evidence of sabotage was fabricated by railroad employees who arrived on the scene in August. Both sides offered witnesses to support their theory of the crime, including some who said they saw the employees tampering with the rails. Others contradicted that testimony by stating that they had spent the whole night at the site of the displaced rail and that there was no tampering.

The presiding judge listened to all the testimony, reviewed the evidence, and then determined that the plaintiffs had failed to prove their case. He awarded judgment in favor of Southern Pacific, with attorney's fees to be paid by the plaintiffs. That had a chilling effect on other lawsuits.

In the end, three different investigations concluded that the wreck of the "City of San Francisco" was the result of sabotage: investigations by the FBI, the Interstate Commerce Commission, and the Southern Pacific Railroad. The case for sabotage was established, but not the identity of the culprit.

With a legal victory assigning sabotage as the cause of the derailment, the railroad showed little compassion in dealing with survivors of the crash. For example, one of the passengers who had been jolted by the speed of the train prior to the accident, F. S. Foote, persisted against the railroad for financial assistance in paying his medical bills. He had suffered a broken jaw, a broken sternum, four cracked ribs, internal hemorrhaging, a concussion, and a punctured lung. Eventually Southern Pacific paid $7,500, which didn't fully cover his medical bills. They also sent him a check for five dollars, with a note explaining that while they refused to refund his regular fare for the journey, they were refunding the full amount of the additional premium he had paid to ride on the "City of San Francisco" as an act of goodwill. They added that they hoped to have the pleasure of serving him in the future.[12]

By disclaiming responsibility for the accident, the Southern Pacific minimized their payments to victims. Still, the railroad suffered substantial financial loss from the complete destruction of five of their top-of-the-line railcars, the collapse of their bridge, and the massive cost of cleanup, repair, and investigation.

So who committed this act of terror? In the most thorough account written about the tragedy, and with full access to Southern Pacific investigative records, Don DeNevi leaves this tantalizing clue in the one-page conclusion of his book *Tragic Train*:

"Although the Southern Pacific Company is prepared to pay the original $10,000 reward for information leading to an arrest and conviction, it can be confided that among retired as well as current railroad detectives one man stands out above all the others as the chief suspect. For nearly 40 years officials knew 'intuitively' that one of their own employees was the guilty party and that he probably acted alone. O'Connell, as well as all the other chief special agents who followed, investigated and reinvestigated this man. But, as much as their intuitive processes sensed that he was the mass killer, they could not come up with one single scrap of evidence for an arrest. That fellow is now dead, and it may be that he carried the final answer to his grave."[13]

His name has never been disclosed to the public.

CHAPTER 7

1940: THE TACOMA NARROWS BRIDGE

THE HUMAN COST OF TRAGEDY

"'I decided I'd like to get a little fun out of it,' [so he] paid the 10-cent [pedestrian] toll and strolled onto the rolling bridge.

"'After walking to the tower on the other side and back I decided to cross it again. It was swaying quite a bit. About the time I got to the center, the wind started blowing harder and, suddenly, I was thrown flat. A car came up about that time. The driver got out, walking and crawling on the other side. We didn't have time for any conversation.

"'Time after time I was thrown completely over the railing. When I tried to get up, I was knocked flat again. Chunks of concrete were breaking up and rolling around. The knees were torn out of my pants, and my knees were cut and torn.

"'I don't know how long it took to get back. It seemed like a lifetime. During the worst parts, the bridge twisted so far that I could see the Coast Guard boat in the water beneath.

"'As soon as I got off the bridge, I became sick. So, I went to the

The Tacoma Narrows Bridge.

home of a cousin and laid down for a while. I've been on plenty of roller coasters, but the worst was nothing compared to this.

"'When I got back, I remembered the bridge man had said something about paying a dime each way. I mentioned it to him.

"'He said, "Skip it."'"[1]

This is an account by Winfield Brown, a twenty-five-year-old college student, who, on November 7, 1940, heard that the new Tacoma Narrows Bridge was undulating in high winds and decided to try it out.

A new design for the road deck, which used plate girders instead of trusses, varied significantly from the standard practices of the era. Far less rigid than a truss deck, the bridge was unusually susceptible to the frequent winds in the area. As the wind passed over and under the deck, a rolling motion began from end to end that caused alternating halves of the center span between the towers to rise and fall by up to ten feet. This motion was disorienting to drivers and pedestrians alike. Some reported that while crossing the bridge, an approaching car would disappear into a trough and then reappear as the wave lifted it back up. It was very much like being in a boat on the ocean, bobbing up and down on the rolling waves, except that

Steel tie-down cables anchoring the bridge.

they were trying to cross a thin, steel-and-concrete deck 195 feet in the air above 200 feet of water!

While many were put off by this motion, others came just to experience the ride. It was like a family roller coaster ride for a fifty-cent fare. Others simply endured the rolling because they needed to get across the Narrows. While people talked and speculated about the motion, almost no one expressed fear, because they assumed the bridge was strong and flexible enough to absorb this motion without damage. After all, its primary architect, Leon Moisseiff, had designed it to withstand winds up to 120 miles per hour, so anything less than that should be safe.

On-site engineers took some modest steps to stabilize the bridge. This included adding steel anchor cables from the bridge deck to fifty-ton concrete blocks on the ground near the shore, but the cables snapped soon after installation. They next tried adding hydraulic dampers between the towers and the deck to absorb some of the motion, but the seals were damaged by sandblasting prior to painting the bridge, so this also proved ineffective. Finally, cable stays were extended from the main towers down to the bridge deck to provide additional support to the suspenders. Unfortunately, these had little effect on the longitudinal rolling. A consulting engineer from the University of Washington, professor Burt Farquharson, suggested that deflector vanes should be installed along the outer edges of the deck system to provide aerodynamic streamlining to the wind flow above and below the deck, also drilling holes through the road deck at strategic places along the center span to allow air to pass through. Both ideas held promise but were not yet implemented by a stormy November day in 1940.

While the bridge had experienced far stronger winds than the forty-two-mile-per-hour speed of November 7, this day was unusual in that the wind was blowing steadily and from a different direction than usual. Although far less than the 120 miles per hour the bridge was designed for, the wind across the peninsula was such that the rise and fall of the deck was far greater than previously experienced. And then a new phenomenon began: the bridge deck started twisting from side to side, in addition to the end-to-end movement.

This new pattern was so alarming that Clark Eldridge, the Washington State Toll Bridge Authority project engineer who had been responsible for building the bridge, was called to the scene:

"'I was in my office about a mile away, when word came that the bridge was in trouble. At about 10 o'clock Mr. Walter Miles called from his office for me to come look at the bridge, that it was about to go.

"'The center span was swaying wildly, it being possible first to see the entire bottom side as it swung into a semi-vertical position and then the entire roadway.

"'I observed that all traffic had been stopped and that several people were coming off the bridge from the easterly side span. I walked to tower No. 5 and out onto the main span to about the quarter point observing conditions. The main span was rolling wildly. The deck was tipping from the horizontal to an angle approaching forty-five degrees. The entire span appeared to be twisting about a neutral point at the center of the span in somewhat the manner of a corkscrew.

"'At tower No. 5, I met Professor Farquharson, who had his camera set up and was taking pictures. We remained there for a few minutes and then decided to return to the east anchorage warning people who were approaching to get off the span.

"'At that time, it appeared that should the wind die down, the span would perhaps come to rest, and I resolved that we would immediately proceed to install a system of cables from the piers to the roadway level in the main span to prevent any recurrence. . . .'"[2]

The urgent question at that moment was whether the wind would die down.

FATEFUL CHOICES

POLITICAL DRAMA—A LESS-EXPENSIVE DESIGN

There had long been interest in building a bridge to span the Tacoma Narrows, south of Seattle. Though the Narrows was just a mile wide, across a narrowing of the Puget Sound, a bridge could shorten the driving distance from Tacoma on the west side of the sound to Gig Harbor on the east side from 107 miles to just eight. That would shave two hours and fifteen minutes off a typical drive. While there was a ferry boat in the area, its capacity was limited, and the schedule infrequent. A bridge would allow unrestricted travel across the Narrows even in bad weather that precluded ferry service.

A bridge would also shorten the travel time between the US Navy's Bremerton Naval Shipyard, on the east side of the Kitsap Peninsula, and the US Army's McChord Air Base, at the southwest corner of the sound, by more than an hour. Accordingly, both the army and navy expressed interest in having a bridge to shorten their response time in emergencies.

Active study of the engineering challenges began in the early 1920s, with an original proposal to build a triple-span, balanced-cantilever, through-truss bridge that would be strong enough to carry both automobile traffic and railroad trains. Washington State engineers thought they could pattern the bridge after the Carquinez

Strait Bridge, completed in 1927, that spanned an inlet of the San Francisco Bay in California.

But the cost of steel was judged too expensive to justify the relatively light traffic that was expected in Washington, so the project was set aside.

By the mid-1930s, the federal government was making funds available to stimulate employment amidst the Great Depression, and interest in a bridge peaked. The Washington State legislature authorized the Washington Toll Bridge Authority to activate the project. A two-tower suspension bridge was substituted for the cantilever design to reduce cost. Even so, it was known from the beginning that early tolls could not pay for the cost of construction and maintenance, so the Toll Bridge Authority sought $11 million in funding from the Federal Public Works Administration.

With a positive response from the FPWA, Washington State engineer Clark Eldridge drafted the initial design of a new suspension bridge that included a set of twenty-five-foot-deep trusses to stiffen the roadway across the entire span of the bridge. This was like the design of other large suspension bridges in major US cities. The estimated cost of this traditional design was $11 million. Before contracts could be let out to bid, however, Leon Moisseiff, a noted New York area bridge designer, petitioned the FPWA to build the bridge for less money using an alternate design. He asserted that using a box-girder design to support the roadway, rather than Eldridge's truss structure, would save more than $4 million in construction costs. It would also provide a more attractive profile to the road deck. Since Moisseiff was considered one of the nation's most eminent design engineers, the FPWA insisted that Moisseiff's design be accepted with him as the lead designer. This was unconventional, but with money difficult to come by, Washington State accepted.

Once in charge of the project, Moisseiff made several critical decisions to save money:

(1) Because of expected light traffic, he decided to create a two-lane road deck, rather than the traditional four lanes of most bridges

of the era. This meant that the deck would be very narrow relative to the length of the spans.

(2) The proposed towers of the bridge had a very narrow profile relative to the length of the bridge. He also reduced the size of the concrete piers that the towers would rest on, compared to Eldridge's design.

(3) He decided to use an eight-foot box-girder design, rather than the twenty-five-foot steel truss design advocated by Eldridge, to stiffen and support the road deck. This substantially reduced the weight and profile of the road deck, giving it less mass to resist wind loads. It also presented a flat vertical surface to the wind on the side of the plate girder rather than the open architecture of the truss design that would have allowed wind to pass through the structure.

When Moisseiff's design was presented to the Washington State Highway Department, they protested, calling "Moisseiff's plan 'fundamentally unsound.' The design would make the bridge proportionally lighter and narrower than any ever built, they said, 'in the interests of economy and cheapness.'"[3]

After a study by outside consultants, it was recommended that the piers be enlarged to the size originally recommended by Eldridge. The rest of Moisseiff's design was accepted, and construction began on November 23, 1938. By January 1940, the towers were completed and spinning of the cables commenced. By May 1940, the steel floor system was completed, and workers started pouring concrete across the roadway. It was an aggressive construction schedule that brought cheers from residents on both sides of the Narrows.

Still, it was not without controversy. From almost the first moment that the plate girder structure was complete, it started reacting to the winds. Many of the workers suffered from motion sickness while doing the necessary work of construction. On-site engineers hoped that the pouring of concrete would stiffen the deck to the point that it would stop rolling, but that was not to be. Workers called the bridge "Galloping Gertie," a name previously assigned to a suspension bridge built in 1849 across the Ohio River in Wheeling, West Virginia. Ominously, that earlier bridge collapsed in a windstorm in 1854.

That earlier history was forgotten on July 1, 1940, when the new Tacoma Narrows Bridge was opened to traffic for the first time. It was a grand celebration, attended by thousands of people and government officials. This was the third longest bridge in the world, and its narrow deck and tall towers graced the harbor with a beautiful profile that promised prosperity for the people of Washington State. Many judged it the most beautiful bridge in existence.

But even on its birthday, the bridge deck rolled in the wind, making for an interesting ride for the officials who made the first trip across the bridge. In the weeks that followed, people struggled to find the proper words to describe the experience of crossing the bridge. The words they used to describe the motion included:

"Gallop, wave, undulation, up and down, breathing, crests and troughs, peaks and valleys, rising and falling, roller coaster, vertical oscillation, and vertical flexibility.

"The roadway sometimes bounced in a wind of only three or four mph. Often, several waves of two to three feet (and on a few occasions up to five feet) would roll from one end of the center span to the other. There seemed to be no correlation between wind speed and the size of the waves. Sometimes the half-mile-long center span would 'bounce' for a few moments then stop. Other times the waves lasted for six or even eight hours."[4]

In retrospect, it seems incredible that few people, including engineers, thought the bridge was at risk from this previously unheard-of amount of flexing.

CONCERNS FROM WORKERS

Not everyone was okay with the flexing. Workers on the bridge had noted the small footprint of the towers relative to other bridges that they had worked on. They also expressed concern about the flexing and rolling in the wind and many had taken bets on how long the bridge would survive. The on-site engineers were anxious to calm the rolling for comfort's sake, but without undue concern for the integrity of the bridge itself. For example, on November 6, 1940, Clark Eldridge was completing work orders for the aerodynamic cowling that was hoped would calm the bridge.

Also on November 6, a Tacoma-area high school student, Carol Peacock, was asked to let her imagination run wild in order to write an essay for her journalism class. Trying to come up with a spectacular headline, she chose the remarkably foreshadowing title, "What If the Tacoma Narrows Bridge Collapses?" She turned her essay in to her teacher on the morning of November 7, 1940.

VICTIMS AND HEROES

November 7, 1940

Ruby Jacox had the following experience while crossing the bridge in a delivery truck on November 7, 1940: "'All of a sudden, the bridge began to rock. We were afraid the truck would turn over so we . . . jumped out. We could only crawl on our hands and knees and got about 10 feet away when the truck fell over.

"'We crawled along hanging onto the ridge of the center of the roadway. Just to keep our courage up we never stopped talking. Chunks of the concrete burst out of the bridge deck as it swayed, groaned, and buckled. I fell dozens of times on the pavement.

"'I was ready to give up, but he (Mr. Hagen) just dragged me along by the shoulder. One of the lampposts just did miss my head. Sometimes I was sure we'd never get off the bridge.

"'I kept thinking that this bridge was something that couldn't break. It had been inspected by government engineers. And experts had planned it so it would stand any strain.'"5

Unfortunately, Ruby Jacox's confidence in the experts who had designed the bridge was misplaced. When she and Arthur Hagen

A still photograph from the morning of the bridge collapse.

drove their delivery truck onto the bridge, they had no idea how close they were to catastrophe. Fortunately, as they crawled toward the end of the rolling and twisting span, exhausted from the struggle, two bridge workers backed their truck partway onto the bridge and quickly hauled Jacox and Hagen aboard and drove them to safety. Jacox was covered in bruises and spent the night in a hospital recovering from what she described as "'terrific nervous shock.'"[6]

$6 MILLION DESTROYED

At approximately 11:00 A.M., large chunks of concrete fell from the bridge. Just minutes later, a 600-foot section of the bridge broke free from the cable suspenders that attached to the main cables and fell 195 feet to the turbulent water below. Observers noted that by then, the bridge was twisting wildly: at one point the sidewalk on one side of the bridge was twenty-eight feet higher than the sidewalk on the other side. Unlike all the previous incidents of longitudinal rolling, this time the bridge was both rolling and twisting. It was

A still photograph of the moment of the bridge collapse.

simply too much for the eight-foot carbon steel girders to take. The collapse of the first section started a cascade of failure, as most of the 2,800 feet of the center span fell into the Puget Sound.

Remarkably, the collapse of the bridge was captured on 16-mm color Kodachrome motion picture film by Barney Elliott, the owner of a local camera shop. To fully appreciate the scope of this catastrophe, you can view a compilation of his movie on YouTube.[7]

A total of five photographers were there that day, shooting the collapse in black-and-white still photos as well as 16-millimeter motion picture film. Thus, the failure of "Gallopin' Gertie" is one of the best-documented, best-known engineering failures in modern history.

Professor F. B. "Burt" Farquharson, who had just a few days earlier released potential solutions to stabilizing the bridge, was on the scene taking still photographs and his own movies during the final hours of the bridge:

"'I was the only person on the Narrows Bridge when it collapsed. I arrived at about a quarter to ten o'clock, the bridge was moving in the familiar rippling motion we were studying and seeking to correct.

"'About a half hour later, it started a lateral twisting motion, in addition to the vertical wave. It had never done that before.

"'At least six lamp posts were snapped off while I watched. A few minutes later, I saw a side girder bulge out. But though the bridge was bucking up an angle of 45 degrees, I thought she would be able to fight it out. But, that wasn't to be.

"'I saw the suspenders (vertical cables) snap off and a whole section caved in. The bridge dropped from under me. I fell and broke one of my cameras. The portion where I was had dropped 30 feet when the tension was released.

"'I kneeled on the roadway and stayed to complete the picture.'"[8]

Fortunately, no one was killed in the collapse of the bridge. A small dog, left behind in a car abandoned on the bridge, was so terrified that it bit its would-be rescuers and retreated back into the car, where it couldn't be reached. It fell to its death with the car. A few people were injured from scrapes and falls they incurred while crawling to safety. Remarkably, even with the bridge deck tipping so steeply on its side that some of those crawling their way toward the end could see the water directly below them, they managed to get off the bridge safely.

But the bridge was destroyed. Later analysis showed that the road decks on the remaining spans were damaged beyond repair. Even though the towers had withstood the shock of the collapse, they were twisted and bent. The east tower was bent more than twelve feet toward the east shore, and both towers had experienced such high stress that portions of the steel had buckled, resulting in permanent distortion. Both these massive structures had to be scrapped. Even the main cables had suffered serious damage, with 350 individual strands snapped and jagged on the north cable. Both main cables were unusable.

The aftermath of the bridge collapse.

The only usable elements left were the concrete piers that supported the towers and the earthen ramps that led up to the approaches of the bridge. For all practical purposes, the $6 million Tacoma Narrows Bridge was a total loss for taxpayers.

PROFESSIONAL HEROES: ACTING TO PREVENT FUTURE TRAGEDY

News of the collapse went out to the world immediately. Leon Moisseiff traveled from New York City to Tacoma to assess the damage. When a reporter asked him why the bridge failed, he replied that he was "completely at a loss to explain the collapse," adding, "I'm unable to understand how it could have happened. I've built bridges all over the world for 45 years and never before has anything like this happened."[9] That is shocking, given what we know about bridge design today, but it is actually an interesting insight into the science of engineering at the time. While engineers could successfully calculate the strength of materials needed to support the dead load (weight of the bridge) and live loads (weight of the traffic), and even had insights into resisting wind loads against a static surface (like the side of a building), very little was known about the aerodynamics of wind over and under flat surfaces like the road deck of a suspension bridge. Up until that time, engineers had solved the problem of wind through brute force, using heavy steel or iron trusses to stiffen the bridge and add enough weight to resist turning and rolling. Plus, the open structure of trusses allowed wind to move freely through the

The broken strands of the main cable after the bridge collapse.

supports. But the amount of steel called for in this approach was far greater than was needed to support the live load, so it seemed a prime candidate for reducing weight and cost. That's what drove Moisseiff's new design with the slim profile of the plate girders. They provided more than adequate strength to support the live load, even when it was unevenly distributed, such as when cars were bunched at one end, or on one side of the bridge. His plate girders were also strong enough to resist lateral wind pressure.

Where his design was inadequate was its inability to resist dynamic wind pressure, which occurs when eddies and swirls occur in the air as wind encounters an uneven surface. This swirling motion created a vacuum on one side of the bridge, lifting the span, and downward pressure in other areas, depressing that side. As the bridge deck responded to this uneven loading, it started to oscillate and then quickly synchronized with the vortexes (swirling air pockets) that were affecting it.

Within weeks of the collapse, a distinguished panel of thirty engineers was convened to consider the causes of the failure, with the specific goal of avoiding another catastrophe in existing and future bridges. Their work dramatically advanced the mathematical under-standing of the aerodynamics of bridge design, aided by improved use of wind tunnels to test the bridge under widely varying wind flow patterns.

The first theory advanced for the failure was that of resonance; the vibration induced by the wind came to match the natural res-onance frequency of the bridge. Just as a tuning fork starts vibrat-ing in tune with an adjacent tuning fork, this theory held that the bridge began longitudinal rolling as a result of sympathy with the wind flow pattern. This theory is still cited by some publications as the primary cause of the collapse. But as the panel studied their models and wind tunnel test results, they determined that it was not the correct explanation. Resonance is important in bridge design, and must be dampened, but it was not the primary cause of Gertie's failure.

What their models had instead suggested is that "torsional flut-ter," also known as "aeroelastic flutter," was the primary culprit, al-though the engineers did not have the computing power necessary to fully explain it. Flutter was being studied at the time as it related to aerodynamic studies, primarily in the design of aircraft, but had not been applied to bridge building. It was the twisting force of the aeroelastic flutter that precipitated the collapse. Here's a very simpli-fied explanation of how it worked:

- Because of its small width-to-length ratio of 1:72, the bridge had very little resistance to longitudinal rolling under even small wind loads.
- While the elements of the bridge remained aligned, the rolling was constrained to end-to-end waves. But at approximately one hour before the collapse of the center span, the stress of the longitudinal waves caused one of the suspender cables on the north main cable to slip from its normal position. This caused the suspender to split into two unequal segments, which placed the north side of the road deck slightly out of alignment with

the south side—like when venetian blinds are being lowered and one side ends up shorter than the other.

- Wind passing over this now-uneven surface created eddies in the flow that added a twisting movement to the synchronized up-and-down motion. When the bridge was rolling only from end to end, the structure was able to absorb those fluctuations because of its natural flexibility. When the new twisting force was added to the mix, stresses began to build rapidly, with waves coming from north and south, east and west. When these opposing waves crashed into each other, they created a standing wave that added incredible stress at that point in the structure.

- What Moisseiff and other designers had no concept of at the time was that these motions become self-reinforcing in what is called "self-excited" motion, like a child lifting then dropping her legs at just the right time on a swing set to increase the height of her arc with very little effort. The uneven bridge deck had become an actor in the rolling and twisting of the bridge, redirecting the wind flow-patterns and increasing the amplitude of each succeeding roll and twist.

As these longitudinal and torsional waves reinforced themselves in ever larger swings, they eventually overwhelmed the strength of the materials supporting the roadbed—the concrete began to fracture and explode. Catastrophe was now inevitable.

OLDER BRIDGES REINFORCED, NEW BRIDGES REDESIGNED

Shortly after the panel's report was released, work started on large suspension bridges across the country to reinforce them against wind hazard. For example, more than $3 million was spent adding stiffening and support to the relatively lightweight truss structure under the roadway of the Golden Gate Bridge in San Francisco. In 1943, fourteen-foot-high steel trusses were installed on both sides of the deck of the Bronx Whitestone Bridge in New York, which had an original design similar to the Tacoma Narrows Bridge. Just as important, new bridge designs reverted to the truss structure under the roadway as the preferred way of resisting movement from wind.

In the 1960s, a box-girder design became an option for supporting the road deck. This was an innovative creation of English engineer Gifford Martel that featured a hollow-tube beam made of pre-stressed concrete, or steel, or a combination of the two. It usually has a trapezoidal aerofoil shape, to provide aerodynamic airflows around the beam and avoid oscillation problems. The box-girder design requires far less maintenance, since there are fewer exposed joints and connections than in the traditional truss design.

Perhaps the most significant contribution of the failure of the Tacoma Narrows 1940 bridge is that all large bridges must now pass a rigorous engineering review and wind-tunnel tests before they can be built. This has made suspension bridges safer for the millions of people who cross them every day.

What about the People?

Leon Moisseiff was treated gently by other engineers. They recognized that he was working within the accepted limits of design at the time. His fatal mistake in designing the Tacoma Narrows Bridge was assuming that the plate-girder structure that worked well on short spans would behave the same way on a long span. A gentle and genuine man, his career was nonetheless ended, as public and government officials no longer trusted him with large projects. He spent most of the three years after the collapse helping with studies of the failed bridge, until he passed away of a heart attack in 1943.

Clark Eldridge was bitter after the collapse, since he was assigned much of the blame as the lead onsite engineer. He pushed back against this, saying:

"The men who held the purse strings were the whip-crackers

on the entire project. We had tried-and-true conventional bridge design. We were told we couldn't have the necessary money without using plans furnished by an eastern firm of engineers, chosen by the money-lenders."[10]

He viewed Moisseiff as an interloper who took the project away from the state of Washington to enrich himself and his engineering firm. But Eldridge's name continued to be associated with the failure. With the outbreak of World War II, he quit his job and went to work for the US Navy on the island of Guam in the South Pacific, only to be captured as a prisoner of war by the Japanese. Even in this far-off place he was recognized by a Japanese officer, who said, in broken English, "Tacoma Bridge."

REPLACEMENT BRIDGE(S)

The bridge was gone, but the need for a bridge wasn't. Commuters on both sides of the Puget Sound had been forced to go back to taking a far longer and more expensive route. With the outbreak of World War II, the demand for steel for the war effort made it impossible to proceed with a replacement bridge. When the war ended, a new bridge was designed using Eldridge's original concrete piers, but with their height increased by seventeen feet to keep corrosive salt water from the Narrows from splashing up on the towers. The new bridge was a four-lane design with heavy steel girders supporting the roadway. It is still in service today.

In 2007, a second suspension bridge was completed, parallel to the 1950 bridge. One bridge now provides four lanes of traffic to the Kitsap Peninsula, while the second bridge provides four lanes of traffic from Kitsap to Tacoma. Both bridges use the underdeck heavy-truss girder design. Together they form an elegant pair that is pleasing to the eye and functional as well. Before the second bridge was approved for construction, models of each of the bridges were placed side by side in a wind tunnel to test the effect of airflows with

The two new bridges across the Tacoma Narrows.

two large structures so close together. Only when the designs harmonized was the project approved.

One question remains: What if Clark Eldridge's original design had been implemented in the first place? Modern computer analysis shows that it would have easily stood up to the winds of November 7, 1940, and, like the Golden Gate and other great bridges of the era, would still be carrying traffic across the Puget Sound today.

CHAPTER 8

1963: ITALY'S VAJONT DAM

THE HUMAN COST OF TRAGEDY

Mario Pancini had successfully designed one of the strongest, safest concrete-arch dams in the world: the Vajont Dam, completed in 1959. Rising more than one hundred feet higher than the famed Hoover Dam, the dam formed a sharp V high above the village of Longarone, Italy, in the steep walls of Vajont Canyon. It was a remarkable accomplishment of modern engineering, proved by a catastrophe of unprecedented proportions that left the dam intact in 1963. More than 2,500 people had perished in a fully predictable disaster. Pancini had tried to avoid putting people in such danger, but it had been forced upon him by powerful political interests. After it happened, he was wracked with guilt and overwhelmed by depression, feeling that he had no right to live when so many others had perished. Of the hundreds of people responsible, he was the only one to express public remorse and offer an apology. All the others called it an "act of God" when, in fact, it was anything but.

A modern view of the Vajont Dam.

Pancini was tormented as he struggled to make sense of how his greatest accomplishment had led to such tragedy.

OVERVIEW

As one of the Axis powers in World War II, Italy was the scene of some of the most intense fighting of the war. Like much of the rest of Europe, its economy was devastated by the destruction of combat. As a result, in the years following World War II, the Italian government was always on the lookout for public works projects to put people to work. In the late 1950s, they found the ideal prestige project: building the tallest concrete-arch dam in the world. The new dam was to be sited in the narrow Vajont Gorge at the southern end of the Dolomites. Located sixty miles north of Venice, this project was expected to produce electricity, irrigation, and tourism.

With so much public money to be spent, there was ample opportunity for political graft and corruption to enrich the politicians and contractors who sponsored the project.

FATEFUL CHOICES

Initial site assessments showed a variety of geological defects where the dam was to be built, specifically that it would rest exclusively on ancient limestone beds, which are subject to fracturing under pressure. The height of the dam was specified at 860 feet from base to crest (130 feet taller than Hoover Dam in the United States). A concrete structure of that size and weight would require a stable foundation. A second problem was that the extremely steep slopes of Monte Toc (Mount Toc), which formed one side of the canyon, were subject to landslides. The limestone layers were intermixed with thin clay layers that became slippery when saturated with rainwater. Additionally, these ancient layers of sediment were tilted on a downward-sloping incline toward the base of the valley floor, which increased the likelihood of slippage if the area was inundated by a reservoir.

Despite these hazards, the opportunity to efficiently generate electric power based on the high head of water behind an 860-foot-tall dam was just too tempting. The electricity monopoly for northeastern Italy, "SADE,"[1] pushed for the authority to build the dam. Under intense political pressure, site engineers concluded that the chances of large-scale landslides were extremely rare, given that "areas of weakness were not identified in the three test borings; it was assumed that any shear plane would have a 'chair-like' form that would exert a 'braking effect'; [and] seismic analyses had suggested that the banks consisted of very firm in-situ rock with a high modulus of elasticity."[2]

With these conclusions in writing, SADE secured the necessary permits to continue and with great fanfare started construction of the dam in 1956.

To compensate for the deficiencies in the limestone at the base of the foundation, the dam's designer, Carlo Semanza, and construction engineer Mario Pancini injected a 500-foot grout curtain to stabilize the base and abutments. This effort was successful and allowed construction to proceed. But a large-scale movement of the canyon wall in late 1958 caused a temporary halt in construction. Three new engineering studies again warned that the base of Monte Toc was extremely unstable and would likely collapse if the dam was completed. All three recommended suspension of the project. But SADE ignored these studies and pushed ahead. Instead of responding to the warnings, Semanza and the government agencies that oversaw construction of the project filed lawsuits against journalists for bringing any attention to perceived deficiencies. The charge: "Their reports acted against the common interests of the people." With powerful political protection, construction of the dam continued. The concrete arch structure was completed in October 1959.

It was a remarkable sight to behold. Comparable in height to an eighty-story building, the new dam stood as high as the main structure of the Chrysler Building in New York City. To demonstrate the steepness of the slopes of the canyon walls, consider that the dam is 627 feet wide at the top, but just eighty-nine feet wide at the base. It towers like a very sharp V in the majestic Vajont Canyon, high above the villages below. The dam was designed to impound 316,000 acre-feet of water, approximately ten times greater than the water held by the St. Francis Dam in Los Angeles.

SADE was granted permission to start filling the reservoir early in 1960, and full pool was achieved in 1961. At this point, it was considered likely that all electrical generation in Italy would be nationalized. Semanza was determined to put the dam into full operation, to achieve the highest possible price if the government decided to buy out his company.

But there was a problem—the predicted landslides had started. For example, on November 4, 1961, a small promontory on the eastern shore of the reservoir shuddered and then collapsed into the lake. This produced a large wave that rippled towards the western shore. At the same time, a large fissure appeared on the face of Mount Toc, above the lake. The fissure was three feet wide and 9,000 feet long. This demonstrated the instability of the material on the eastern shore.

In response to this, SADE decided that the best way to stabilize the mountain was to expose it to changing water levels and pressure. It was hoped that in doing so, the rock and clay would adjust through moderate movements until the material reached a new point of equilibrium in the environment of the reservoir. Thus, the lake was raised and held steady for a time, then lowered, then raised slightly, then lowered again. Each of these adjustments caused movement in the eastern abutment, but none so dramatic as to raise serious alarm.

Still, engineers were so concerned that SADE decided to excavate a large bypass tunnel in Mount Salta on the western shore of the lake. This would allow a second way for water to exit the reservoir if the lake was ever divided into two parts by a landslide. It was a very dramatic cure for a problem that didn't yet exist.

By November 1962, the water level was raised again to nearly full pool in anticipation of the nationalization of SADE. From Semanza's point of view, it was critical that the dam be labeled operational to get the maximum selling price. If it was labeled "under test" or "non-operational," the government could purchase the dam at a fraction of its operational value. Even though there were extremely disturbing signs of instability on the Monte Toc side of the reservoir, SADE pressed for operational status. It was granted, despite the appearance of cracks (from ground movement) in the homes on the slope of Mount Toc, above the waterline. Paint splintered on the walls, doors warped, and a brand-new school that SADE had built was so damaged by earth movement that it was deemed unfit for use. Even a brand-new road built by SADE around the shore of the new lake shifted out of its original alignment, making travel difficult.

DANGER NEAR THE SHORELINE

What is remarkable, in retrospect, is that few people seemed to have concerns about the integrity of the dam in the event of a large landslide, even those living below the dam. The most concerned group were those whose villages were near the shores of the new lake *above* the dam, particularly in the towns of Erto and Casso. Their primary fear was that people living on the eastern shore could be hurt if the land underneath them started sliding, particularly since landslides saturated with water move at incredible speeds. Their second concern was that a large landslide into the reservoir could create a tsunami wave that would wash up and over their towns. The small slides already experienced prior to the fall of 1962 had created waves that came worryingly close to the footings of buildings on the shore of the lake. These concerns became so great that in early September 1963, the mayor of Erto sent a letter to SADE, urging them to lower the level of the lake. He pleaded that his fellow citizens felt as if they were living in a nightmare because of constant concern that a wave could destroy their lives and their property. SADE did not respond to his letter.

By this point, crews at the dam were near panic. The rocky slope on Monte Toc was sliding down towards the lake, sometimes as much as seventy feet per day. It was obvious that if nothing was done, the ramifications would be deadly. The problem was trying to figure out how to manipulate the level of the reservoir to minimize the chance of a landslide. The thinking was that if the water level dropped too quickly, it would be a shock to the slide-prone area and precipitate a rapid collapse. If the water level was lowered too slowly, and an earthquake occurred, the inevitable tsunami wave was far more likely to cause serious damage. There was even the risk of some water overtopping the dam. So SADE began lowering the level of the lake gradually, but at exactly the rate that maximized electrical power generation—a very convenient event for SADE.

Tuesday, October 8, 1963, was a day of increasing anxiety.

Movement of the eastern abutment was so severe that trees were falling over. The road built around the lake was completely unusable.
By late morning, SADE sent out a warning that all people living on
the eastern shore should evacuate the area immediately. They also
suggested that residents of Casso at the upper end of the lake move
to higher ground since "landslides can create frightening waves in
the whole lake." They were thoughtful enough to suggest that swim-
mers would be particularly vulnerable to such waves.

UNINTENDED CONSEQUENCES

WEDNESDAY, OCTOBER 9, 1963—CATASTROPHE!

At 10:39 P.M., the entire slope of Monte Toc collapsed into the
reservoir in a mighty explosion. 800 million cubic feet of clay and
limestone displaced an equal amount of water in the reservoir. This
gigantic slide moved at a rate of sixty miles per hour, sliding into the
lake in just forty-five seconds.

The effect was completely unexpected—the water in the lake
rose more than 600 feet above the top of the dam, and then fell
over the front. This crushing waterfall created a shock wave at the
base of the dam more powerful than that of the atomic bomb exploded at Hiroshima, Japan. Landing in such a narrow canyon, the
displaced air blasted down the canyon, obliterating everything in its
path—buildings, trees, rock, and people. Nearly all the bodies of the
victims of the shock wave were found naked, their clothes blown
off by the force. Of course, the water itself quickly followed, in a
mighty wave that scoured away all remnants of human habitation in
the narrow gorge. Once the water reached the mouth of the canyon,
it flattened out into a wider wave, but that was little comfort to the
2,500 people who were killed by the flood.

The community of Longarone and its satellite villages were hard-
est hit, with more than 80 percent casualties. Above the dam, the
tsunami wave created by the landslide destroyed the town of Casso

The aftermath of the landslide, with the still-intact Vajont Dam visible in the center bottom of the photograph.

as well as the lower buildings in Erto. Survivors who witnessed the landslide said it was as if the entire side of the mountain disappeared into a giant white cloud. At first, they thought the cloud was dust, but it was the water of the lake rising 600 feet into the air. It was an epic disaster, but it had been both foreseeable and preventable.

The Dam Survives!

Perhaps the most remarkable part of the story is that the Vajont Dam survived the catastrophe. It was so well-engineered that it resisted the incredible increase in force and held firm as the water overtopped it. The highway across the top of the dam was destroyed, ripped away by the force of the water passing over the concrete. But the dam itself held. In fact, it is still there today. It appears as a huge white V when seen from below. It is an odd structure, sitting high above the now almost completely earth-filled canyon behind the dam where the reservoir once was. So massive was the amount of material sloughed by the landslide that it is impossible to excavate. Now a large plain shelters behind the dam, 600 feet above the valley below. Two small lakes have formed upstream from the slide above the dam. As rain falls and the level in these lakes rises, water is released through the original outlet tunnel as well as through the second tunnel built on the other side, high up on the canyon wall. Looking at the dam from below, one is struck by the beautiful waterfalls rushing from both sides of the mountain, below the crest of the dam.

VICTIMS AND FIRST-RESPONDER HEROES

In 2013, BBC News correspondent Mark Duff interviewed several survivors of the catastrophe for the fiftieth anniversary of the collapse of the dam in 1963. Here is the story shared by Micaela Colletti, one of just thirty children who survived from the town of Longarone and the only survivor in her family. Her father, mother, sister, and grandmother all perished in the flood. She was just twelve years old on the night of October 9, 1963:

"'I heard what I thought was a thunderclap. It was incredibly loud. My granny came into my room and said she was going to close all the shutters because a storm was coming.

"'At exactly the same moment all the lights went out and I heard a sound, impossible to describe properly. The closest thing I've ever heard to it is the sound of metal shop shutters rolling down, crashing shut, but this was a million, a billion times worse.

"'I felt my bed collapsing, as if there was a hole opening beneath me and an irresistible force dragging me out. I couldn't do anything. I had no idea what was happening.'

"[Micaela] was hurled more than [1,000 feet] through the air and buried.

"'When they pulled me out there was a popping sound, like when you open a bottle, and someone said 'We've found another old one.' I was just 12 but I was covered in mud and completely black and must have looked like an old woman.

"'I remember I was on the shoulders of the only fireman from the town to survive and he kept stumbling over these bright, incredibly white, translucent rocks and I kept asking him to put me down, but he wouldn't.

"'. . . There was this huge moon so close and so bright it scared me. I felt if I stretched out my hand, I could touch it. I've never seen a moon like it, so close and so huge.

"'Then they put me in a car, and I heard someone crying and I suddenly realized it was me.'"[3]

Micaela laments the fact that the bodies of her mother, sister, and grandmother were never found. Her father's remains were identified, and he was buried, but the site is unknown. Markers commemorate the deaths of her family members, but their experience in death is unknown.

A resident of Casso who lived above the reservoir reported that he was awakened at 10:15 P.M. by "a very loud and continuous sound of rolling rocks." But this did not disturb him since there had been lots of slide activity in the area. It was raining hard. "About 10:40 P.M. a very strong wind struck the house, breaking the window panes. Then the house shook violently; there was a very loud rumbling noise. Soon afterward the roof of the house was lifted so that the rain and rocks came hurtling into the room on the second floor in what seemed like half a minute. He had jumped up and out of bed to open the door and leave when the roof collapsed onto the bed. The wind suddenly died down and everything in the valley was quiet."[4] He had experienced the shock wave that was created by the tsunami wave, which was created by the crashing of the landslide into the reservoir.

The 600-foot wall of water that overtopped the canyon crashed onto the valley floor at approximately 10:40 P.M. Three minutes later, the shock wave blasted the canyon below the dam at supersonic speed, smashing out windows and shaking the earth with tremors. The destruction caused by the blast of air, followed by the jet of water, was incredible. For example, the massive steel I-beams in the underground powerhouse were "twisted like a corkscrew and sheared."[5] The shock wave was quickly followed by a 230-foot-high flood that tore down the valley. It destroyed nearly everything in the village of Longarone in the mouth of the canyon, except for a church bell tower, which was only partially damaged. Then the flood wave broadened out before turning into the Piave Valley, where it wrecked the villages of Cadissago, Pirago, and Villanova. Unlike the St. Francis flood that took many hours to play out as it worked its way to the ocean, the destruction of the Vajont flood ended quickly, mostly because the area affected was remote and lightly populated.

So fierce was the force of the landslide, shock wave, and crashing of water over the face of the dam that seismic tremors were recorded at earthquake stations over a wide area of Europe, even as far north as Brussels, Belgium. These stations established that the recorded seismic waves were the *result* of the landslide, not its cause. That was an important distinction in ruling out an earthquake as the primary cause of the disaster.

The disruption in power that caused a blackout just moments after the water and shock wave destroyed the powerhouse was the first indication to the rest of Italy that something was wrong.

As reports flooded in, rescue workers started making their way to the devastated area. Local Italian resources were supplemented by US Army helicopters and paratroopers on assignment in Italy who aided in rescue efforts and brought supplies into the devastated areas. Taking more than 300 flights, they ferried out more than 4,000 survivors. It was because of the earnest and heroic efforts of Italians and Americans working side by side that the surviving victims were saved from further suffering. Through the help of those who rushed to the scene, the survivors were soon given medical attention, food, and temporary shelter. Their villages had been destroyed, but they were still alive.

PROFESSIONAL HEROES: ACTING TO PREVENT FUTURE TRAGEDY

The owners of the dam quickly declared that the flood was an "act of God," completely unpredictable and not a result of human error or faulty design. This was a hard case to make to the people living in the area. They had warned the government about Monte Toc's instability and had watched as the electric company had manipulated the lake level to try to create a controlled slide. But before an independent investigation could establish cause and responsibility, the disaster was politicized by the Communists, who had opposed the dam from the beginning. They declared the disaster to be the result of greed and mismanagement. Italy's prime minister quickly reacted to this by accusing the Communists of "political profiteering" at the expense of the victims, and then moved to silence the debate. A trial was held, in which a handful of engineers were found negligent. The government never sued the electric company for damages.

The only person to fully accept responsibility was the construction engineer, Mario Pancini, who fell into such despair that he committed suicide. He had tried mightily to prevent tragedy but was unable to resist the political pressure to construct a dam in an area he knew to be unsuitable. For this he paid with his life.

Many of the survivors were relocated to a new village, Vajont, southeast of the mouth of the canyon. Longarone and other villages were rebuilt, offering new housing for those who chose to return. The government also offered loans and subsidies to survivors who wished to start new businesses to revitalize the area. But the corruption continued: most of these subsidies were granted to large industrial concerns that built factories and plants elsewhere in Italy using the credits intended for the flood victims.

Within a few years, almost no one talked about the tragedy—it was an embarrassment to be avoided. It was many decades later that survivors started sharing their stories to keep the memory of that awful night alive. A memorial church designed by the noted

A modern view of the Vajont Dam from the valley below.

architect Giovanni Michelucci was built in Longarone to honor both the victims and the survivors of the tragedy.

Yet, all was not in vain. The Vajont Reservoir tragedy drew international attention to the dangers of building reservoirs in canyons that had steep slopes faced with slide-prone material. It became an additional consideration in properly siting dams to reduce the risk of a tragedy like Vajont.

THE VAJONT DAM TODAY

A pumping station was built on the upside of the dam to draw water from the two small lakes into the outlet tunnels. In 2002, a visitors' center was built at the crest of the dam so tourists could visit the site and see the irony of a huge dam impounding a dry basin that is now covered in vegetation. In 2006, a track and field event entitled "Paths of Remembrance" was inaugurated, allowing runners to go inside some of the tunnels used in construction and originally intended to aid in power generation.

FINAL THOUGHTS

Now that you've read the eight stories in this collection, let's talk about the characters in the stories, their motives, and their reactions. There are four parties in every catastrophe—the people who caused the catastrophe, the people who were harmed by it, the people who acted to rescue and comfort the survivors, and the people who worked hard to prevent it from happening again. With respect to the bad actors in the stories, I believe their motives fell into three categories: malice, greed, and hubris (excessive pride or self-confidence).

MALICE

The saboteur(s) of the "City of San Francisco" in Chapter 6, "1939: Death in the Desert," had an evil motive to move the tracks and intentionally derail the high-speed passenger train. He (or they) had to know that this act would kill and injure innocent people as well as destroy millions of dollars of property. Great suffering was caused in an early act of terror reminiscent of other violent acts, such as the mass shootings of our day.

GREED

Reuben Hatch and Captain James Mason put their own financial interest ahead of the safety of their passengers by overloading the *Sultana* in Chapter 1, "1865: Prisoners on the Mississippi." Thousands were harmed because of their greed. Mason paid for his mistake with his life, but Hatch escaped responsibility—and probably did not even have a guilty conscience, since nothing in his life suggested that he had a conscience at all. The greed of the directors of SADE, the Italian power company behind the construction of the Vajont Dam, led to the fatal shock wave and flood that killed thousands of people, recounted in Chapter 8, "1963: Italy's Vajont Dam." Despite engineering warnings, they silenced critics and forced the dam to be constructed on a site that was known to be unstable. They, too, escaped financial consequences, since by the time the commission's report was released, which labeled the catastrophe an "act of God" when it was anything but, their company had been purchased by the Italian government.

HUBRIS

The other five stories are about men who overestimated their skills and refused to seek critical review of their work.

Sir Thomas Bouch was incompetent in designing bridges, yet his arrogance was so extreme that even after the Tay Bridge disaster, he continued to design similar structures with absolute indifference to the potential harm.

C. R. Rockwood was the incompetent and overconfident engineer who opened the Colorado River to the Imperial Valley without adequate resources or engineering know-how. Once the problem was out of control, he slunk away in disgrace, leaving the herculean task of repair to the civil engineers of the Southern Pacific Railroad, exposing thousands of workers to danger, and consuming the equivalent of nearly $100 million in 2019 dollars to correct the damage caused by his incompetence. I also believe that the United States Congress was a villain in this story. The Imperial Valley was largely owned by the government, but Congress failed to vote to reimburse the railroad for doing repair work that clearly benefited everyone. Theirs was a selfish and punitive action against Southern Pacific's president, E. H. Harriman, whom I view as the hero in the story.

William Mulholland, who had no formal training in engineering, was so confident in his abilities and proud of his abrasive and domineering leadership that he refused to submit his plans to outside review. Building the St. Francis Dam as he did reflects sheer incompetence. But since he answered to no one, the tragedy unfolded. Even though his conscience was tormented by the deaths he had caused, he still refused to accept that his design was in error.

It was engineer Leon Moisseff who arrogantly used his political connections to override other engineers' time-tested design for a new bridge over the Tacoma Narrows. His cheaper design was used instead, and it proved deficient and dangerous from the moment it was open. At least his errors in judgment did not lead to any loss of life. I will say that I can't imagine why anyone ever traveled over that bridge as it undulated from end to end. Why it wasn't shut down the first time a car bucked in the wind is a puzzle I'll never understand.

Finally, Ray Sheldon had the authority to evacuate the workers under his control in the Florida Keys well in advance of the worst hurricane on record, but was too busy playing cards to act with dispatch. The evil part of that story is that some veterans who wanted to go north were prevented from doing so at gunpoint. No wonder Ernest Hemingway declared their deaths in the storm as murder, rather than as accidental.

The motive of malice is beyond my understanding—I don't understand why people who feel they have suffered some wrong think that it's okay for them to take out their vengeance on strangers. It's important to remember that the victims of a catastrophe number far more than those directly injured or killed—their family members and friends carry the emotional scars of losing a loved one for the rest of their lives. Why someone would intentionally cause that kind of pain is beyond me.

Greed is a more familiar motive—people want the power, prestige, and comfort that comes with money, so they take shortcuts and resort to deception and cheating to enrich themselves with the hope that it will turn out okay. Theirs is the sin of indifference.

Hubris strikes closest to home. As a person gains confidence and the respect of others, they come to view that approval as a right, and "believe their own biography," to the point that they look with disdain on others' opinions. Theirs is the sin of pride. They do not wish to intentionally harm others, but their incompetence often assures it. The antidote to hubris is humility. It takes a strong person to keep one's humility in the face of personal success. Humility is not weak—far from it. It is an acknowledgment of one's strength, tempered by an admission of one's inability to foresee all possible outcomes. That's why a successful but humble person welcomes outside review and criticism. It's hard to do, but critical to true success.

The bottom line is that the motive of any of these bad actors didn't really matter to the victims. The harm done was the same.

HEROES

What about the heroes? I have written seventeen books that all talk about heroes—people who act at their own risk to help others. Many of the stories are from history, so I've turned to original documents to learn about the people involved. That's the case in this book, *Catastrophes and Heroes*. In some cases, I have met the individuals face-to-face to help them tell their story, and each meeting has been a signal event in my life. I met men like Colonel Bernie Fisher of the United States Air Force, who earned the Medal of Honor (our highest military award) for placing his life at risk to rescue a downed comrade. I met Rudi Wobbe, one of three German boys who stood up to Adolf Hitler, incurring the full wrath of the mighty Third

Reich in doing so. He was remarkable in his commitment to truth and freedom. And I met Joseph Banks, who struggled to stay alive in the face of impossible odds so that he could bear witness of the courage and goodness of his crewmates on a B-17 bomber in World War II. He has inspired hundreds of thousands of readers. From the events in *Catastrophes and Heroes,* I admire Captain Watson of the *Bostona II,* who saw the burning wreckage of the *Sultana* and immediately set his priorities aside to rescue as many in the freezing water as possible. Once his own boat was overloaded, he sped south to alert other rescuers. I was also particularly moved by the stories of Confederate soldiers who set their prejudices aside to help rescue their former enemies as they struggled in the river. From the story of the collapse of the St. Francis Dam, I admire the "Hello Girls," who operated the telephone exchange in full knowledge that the flood might overtake and kill them. And the story of deputy Eddie Hearne, driving his Cadillac straight towards the oncoming flood while warning people to escape, raised the hair on the back of my neck, particularly when he saw his headlights reflected in the wall of water rushing towards him. It was inspiring to picture train engineer Ed Hecox running more than a mile and a half that desert night to find help for his passengers on the destroyed "City of San Francisco," and the efforts of those who offered medical help, despite their own injuries and pain. Heroes are remarkable, particularly since they are people just like you and me—until an emergency strikes and they reach deep inside their soul to find the courage to face danger and help others.

Think about it this way: the heroes in my books—and all the other heroes in our world—are the exact opposite of the bad actors in their response to tragedy. While malice, greed, and hubris motivated the perpetrators of these disasters, it was kindness, empathy, and courage that motivated the rescuers. Even though I keep trying, I can never fully pay tribute to the heroes' sacrifice and courage.

Finally, there was something new in these stories, at least compared to the leading characters in my previous books: the "professional heroes," who stepped up after each disaster, reviewed the mistakes made, and designed and implemented remedies that may prevent similar disasters from happening again. There is always uncertainty in life, particularly with respect to huge projects like the ones we have discussed, but the fact that the replacement Tay Bridge is still in operation more than 120 years after the collapse of Sir Thomas Bouch's failed design is a testament to the quality of the reforms implemented after that tragedy. Large dams like the St. Francis are now subject to rigorous outside review, and that has saved countless lives. These professional heroes work largely unnoticed and behind the scenes to make the world safer, and we are all in their debt.

I love the stories in this book. I hope you do, too.

JERRY BORROWMAN
October 2019

NOTES

CHAPTER 1—1865: PRISONERS ON THE MISSISSIPPI

1. In Chester D. Berry, *Loss of the* Sultana *and Reminiscences of the Survivors*, 36.
2. In Gene Salecker, *Disaster on the Mississippi: The* Sultana *Explosion, April 27, 1865*, 30.
3. Sally M. Walker, *Sinking the* Sultana, 94–95.
4. In Berry, *Loss of the* Sultana, 29–31.
5. Despite the name and the association with Mississippi River steamboats, this was not the famous author Mark Twain.

CHAPTER 2—1879: SCOTLAND'S TAY RAILWAY BRIDGE

1. See Robin Lumley, *Tay Bridge Disaster: The People's Story*, location 374.
2. "HMS" stands for "Her Majesty's Ship," a designation given to ships of the Royal Navy. "RMS" stands for Royal Mail Ship, which is a designation assigned to privately owned ships like the RMS *Titanic* that carried mail under contract with the British postal service.
3. 500 British pounds in 1879, adjusted for inflation, is equal to approximately $70,000 US dollars in 2019.
4. In John Prebble, *The High Girders: The Story of the Tay Bridge Disaster*, 110.
5. Prebble, *The High Girders*, 124.
6. Lumley, *Tay Bridge Disaster*, locations 3501–3510.
7. Lumley, *Tay Bridge Disaster*, location 3238.
8. Peter Lewis, *Beautiful Railway Bridge of the Silvery Tay: Britain's Worst Engineering Disaster Revisited*, 129–30.

CHAPTER 3—1906: HARRIMAN FIGHTS THE COLORADO

1. See William deBuys and Joan Myers, *Salt Dreams: Land and Water in Low-Down California*, 65. The Salton Trough is considered to be the northern extension of the Gulf of California (see *Salt Dreams*, 112–14).

2. Marc Reisner, *Cadillac Desert: The American West and Its Disappearing Water*, 123.
3. See Kim Stringfellow, *Greetings from the Salton Sea: Folly and Intervention in the Southern California Landscape, 1905–2005.*
4. Stringfellow, *Greetings from the Salton Sea.*
5. Silt is fine sand and clay that is suspended in river water while the current is strong, but is deposited as sediment when the water slows. As the Colorado River works its way through the sandstone deserts of Utah and the Grand Canyon of Arizona, it erodes an enormous amount of sediment, leading to an extremely heavy silt load.
6. George Kennan, *E. H. Harriman: Railroad Czar*, 2:29.
7. Kennan, *E. H. Harriman*, 139–41.
8. More than $50 million in 2019 inflation-adjusted dollars.

CHAPTER 4—1928: MULHOLLAND'S ST. FRANCIS DAM

1. Jon Wilkman, *Floodpath: The Deadliest Man-Made Disaster of 20th-Century America and the Making of Modern Los Angeles*, 98–99.
2. Marc Reisner, *Cadillac Desert: The American West and Its Disappearing Water*, 93.
3. In Wilkman, *Floodpath*, 50.
4. M. M. O'Shaugnessy, *Hetch Hetchy: Its Origins and History*, 68.
5. J. David Rogers, "A Man, a Dam, and a Disaster: Mulholland and the St. Francis Dam," 32.
6. In Michelle E. Buttellman, "Historic Headlines: Remembering the St. Francis Dam Disaster," *The Signal.*
7. Los Angeles County coroner's inquest transcript, 178; quoted by Wilkman in *Floodpath*, 85.
8. John Nichols, *Images of America: St. Francis Dam Disaster*, 21.
9. Wilkman, *Floodpath*, 96.
10. Wilkman, *Floodpath*, 98.
11. See Wilkman, *Floodpath*, 119–20.
12. See Nichols, *Images of America: St. Francis Dam Disaster*, 6.
13. In Nichols, *Images of America: St. Francis Dam Disaster*, 16.
14. In Nichols, *Images of America: St. Francis Dam Disaster*, 208.
15. In Les Standiford, *Water to the Angels: William Mulholland, His Monumental Aqueduct, and the Rise of Los Angeles*, 8.
16. J. David Rogers, "A Man, a Dam, and a Disaster," 86.

CHAPTER 5—1935: THE OVER-SEA RAILROAD

1. Phil Scott, *Hemingway's Hurricane: The Great Florida Keys Storm of 1935*, 172–73.
2. Les Standiford, *Last Train to Paradise: Henry Flagler and the Spectacular Rise and Fall of the Railroad that Crossed an Ocean*, 94–95.
3. Pat Parks, *The Railroad That Died at Sea: The Florida East Coast's Key West Extension*, 9.

4. In Standiford, *Last Train to Paradise*, 204.

5. In Standiford, *Last Train to Paradise*, 205, 206.

6. See Jan Sjostrom, "A Titanic Legacy: Exhibit Explores Life of Henry Flagler," *Palm Beach Daily News*.

7. Willie Drye, *Storm of the Century: The Labor Day Hurricane of 1935*, 82.

8. Thomas Neil Knowles, *Category 5: The 1935 Labor Day Hurricane*, 173–74.

9. Knowles, *Category 5*, 177.

10. Knowles, *Category 5*, 176.

11. Standiford, *Last Train to Paradise*, 231–32.

12. Scott, *Hemingway's Hurricane*, 141.

13. Scott, *Hemingway's Hurricane*, 178–79.

14. Scott, *Hemingway's Hurricane*, 170.

CHAPTER 6—1939: DEATH IN THE DESERT

1. Don DeNevi, *Tragic Train: "The City of San Francisco": The Development and Historic Wreck of a Streamliner*, 45–48.

2. In Charles McAvoy, *Journey: The Travels, Tragedies, and Triumphs*, 68.

3. The amount of $2 million in 1936 would be equivalent to nearly $37 million in 2019.

4. See Southern Pacific Company, *Our Dining Car Recipes*.

5. "Southern Pacific Passenger Trains: The City of San Francisco."

6. See DeNevi, *Tragic Train*, 9–13.

7. DeNevi, *Tragic Train*, 42–43.

8. DeNevi, *Tragic Train*, 53, 59.

9. In DeNevi, *Tragic Train*, 60.

10. DeNevi, *Tragic Train*, 59.

11. See DeNevi, *Tragic Train*, 149, 166.

12. See Howard Hickson, "Recalling a Train Wreck."

13. DeNevi, *Tragic Train*, 167.

CHAPTER 7—1940: THE TACOMA NARROWS BRIDGE

1. Winfield Brown, in Washington State Department of Transportation, "Tacoma Narrows Bridge: Eyewitness Accounts."

2. Clark Eldridge, in "Tacoma Narrows Bridge: Eyewitness Accounts."

3. Richard S. Hobbs, *Catastrophe to Triumph: Bridges of the Tacoma Narrows*, 11.

4. Hobbs, *Catastrophe to Triumph*, 19.

5. Ruby Jacox, in "Tacoma Narrows Bridge."

6. Ruby Jacox, in "Tacoma Narrows Bridge."

7. See "Tacoma Narrows Bridge Collapse 'Gallopin' Gertie,'" YouTube. Most copies of the film show the bridge oscillating approximately 50 percent faster than in real time, due the assumption that it was shot at 24 frames per second rather than the actual 16 fps. When properly adjusted, the film shows the center span rising and falling 12 times per minute (once every five seconds) at the time of the collapse, which corresponds to the timing measured by witnesses at the scene. It's important to note both the rolling motion and

the twisting motion, since it was this combination that precipitated the collapse.

8. F. B. "Burt" Farquharson, in "Tacoma Narrows Bridge."
9. In Rob Carson, *Masters of Suspension: The Men and Women Who Bridged the Tacoma Narrows Once Again.*
10. In Hobbs, *Catastrophe to Triumph*, 89.

CHAPTER 8—1963: ITALY'S VAJONT DAM

1. SADE is the acronym for the Società Adriatica di Elettricità (Adriatic Electricity Company).
2. David Pettley, "The Vajont (Vaiont) Landslide"; paragraphing altered.
3. Mark Duff, "Italy Vajont anniversary: Night of the 'tsunami.'"
4. See George A. Kiersch, "The Worst Dam Disaster in the World (Vaiont)," in *Mineral Information Service*, Vol. 18, no. 7 (July 1965): 129–41.
5. See Kiersch, "The Worst Dam Disaster in the World (Vaiont)," 129–41.

BIBLIOGRAPHY

Berry, Chester D. *Loss of the* Sultana *and Reminiscences of the Survivors: A History of a Disaster.* Lansing, MI: Darius D. Thorpe, 1892.

Buttelman, Michelle E. "Historic Headlines: Remembering the St. Francis Dam Disaster." *The Signal.* Available at https://scvhistory.com/sg031101.htm. Accessed 21 October 2019.

Carson, Rob. *Masters of Suspension: The Men and Women Who Bridged the Tacoma Narrows Once Again.* Tacoma, WA: News Tribune, 2007.

Cowan, Wes, Kaiama Glover, and Zuberi Tukufu. *History Detectives Special Investigations—Civil War Sabotage.* Final Transcript.

D'Angelo, Alexa N. "FBI offers $300K reward 20 years after Arizona train derails." *Arizona Republic,* 6 April 2015. Available at https://www.azcentral.com /story/news/local/arizona/2015/04/06/fbi-arizona-train-derailment-abrk /25372511/. Accessed 10 October 2019.

deBuys, William and Joan Myers. *Salt Dreams: Land and Water in Low-Down California.* Albuquerque: University of New Mexico Press, 2017.

DeNevi, Don. *Tragic Train: "The City of San Francisco": The Development and Historic Wreck of a Streamliner.* Seattle, WA: Superior Publishing, 1977.

Drye, Willie. *Storm of the Century: The Labor Day Hurricane of 1935.* Revised edition. Guilford, CT: Rowman & Littlefield, 2019.

Duff, Mark. "Italy Vajont anniversary: Night of the 'tsunami,'" 10 October 2013. *BBC News* (website). Available at http://www.bbc.com/news/world-europe -24464867. Accessed 10 October 2019.

Goldstone, Bruce. *The Rise and Fall of Galloping Gertie.* New York: McGraw-Hill, 1999.

Hemingway, Ernest. "Who Killed the Vets? A First-Hand Report on the Florida Hurricane." In *New Masses* (magazine), 13 September 1935.

Hickson, Howard. "Recalling a Train Wreck." In *Howard Hickson's Histories* (website). Available at https://www.gbcnv.edu/howh/. Accessed 2 January 2020.

Hobbs, Richard S. *Catastrophe to Triumph: Bridges of the Tacoma Narrows.* Pullman, WA: Washington State University Press, 2006.

Huffman, Alan. *"Sultana": Surviving the Civil War, Prison, and the Worst Maritime*

Disaster in American History. Kindle Edition. New York: Harper Perennial, 2009.

Kennan, George. *E. H. Harriman: Railroad Czar.* Volume 2. New York: Cosimo, 2005.

Kennan, George. *The Salton Sea—An Account of Harriman's Fight with the Colorado River.* New York: Macmillan, 1917.

Kiersch, George A. "The Worst Dam Disaster in the World (Vaiont)." In *Mineral Information Service,* vol. 18, no. 7 (July 1965): 129–41.

Knowles, Thomas Neil. *Category 5: The 1935 Labor Day Hurricane.* Gainesville, FL: University Press of Florida, 2015.

Labaton, Stephen. "F.B.I. Studies Note for Clues on Derailment." *The New York Times,* 11 October 1995. Available at https://www.nytimes.com/1995/10/11/us/fbi-studies-note-for-clues-on-derailment.html. Accessed 26 January 2019.

Lewis, Peter. *Beautiful Railway Bridge of the Silvery Tay: Britain's Worst Engineering Disaster Revisited.* Cheltenham, UK: Tempus Publishing, 2008.

Lincoln, Abraham. *Second Inaugural Address,* 4 March 1865. Available at https://berkleycenter.georgetown.edu/quotes/abraham-lincoln-on-god-and-the-civil-war-in-1865-inaugural-address. Accessed 22 February 2019.

Lumley, Robin. *Tay Bridge Disaster: The People's Story.* Cheltenham, UK: The History Press. Kindle Edition, 2013.

McAvoy, Charles V. *Journey: The Travels, Tragedies, and Triumphs.* Bloomington, IN: Xlibris, 2003.

McLaughlin, Mark. "Nevada Train Wreck: Unsolved Mystery." In "Snowy Range Reflections," *Journal of Sierra Nevada History & Biography,* vol. 6, no 2 (Fall 2015). Tahoe Nugget no. 214, 24 August 2011. Rocklin, CA: Sierra College Press. Available at https://www.sierracollege.edu/ejournals/jsnhb/v6n2/trainwreck.html. Accessed 26 January 2019.

Newell, F. H. "The Salton Sea." In *Annual Report of the Board of Regents of the Smithsonian Institution: Showing the Operations, Expenditures, and Condition of the Institution for the Year Ending June 30, 1907.* Washington, DC: Government Printing Office, 1908.

Nichols, John. *Images of America: St. Francis Dam Disaster.* Charleston, SC: Arcadia Publishing, 2002.

Nunis, Doyce, ed. *The St. Francis Dam Disaster: Revisited.* Los Angeles: Historical Society of Southern California, 1995.

O'Shaugnessy, M. M. *Hetch Hetchy: Its Origins and History.* San Francisco: John J. Newbegin, 1934.

Parks, Pat. *The Railroad That Died at Sea: The Florida East Coast's Key West Extension.* Key West, FL: Langley Press, 1968.

Pettley, David. In *The Landslide Blog* (website). Available at https://blogs.agu.org/landslideblog/2008/12/11/the-vaiont-vajont-landslide-of-1963/. Accessed 9 October 2019.

Prebble, John. *The High Girders: The Story of the Tay Bridge Disaster.* London: Secker and Warburg, 1956.

Preston, Porter J. *The All-American Canal: Report of the All-American Canal Board.* Washington, DC: Government Printing Office, 1920.

Reisner, Marc. *Cadillac Desert: The American West and Its Disappearing Water*, 2nd edition. New York: Penguin, 1993.

Rogers, J. David. "A Man, a Dam, and a Disaster: Mulholland and the St. Francis Dam." In *The St. Francis Dam Disaster: Revisited*. Doyce Nunis, ed. Los Angeles: Historical Society of Southern California, 1995.

Salecker, Gene Eric. *Disaster on the Mississippi: The* Sultana *Explosion, April 27, 1865*. Annapolis, MD: Naval Institute Press, 1996.

Scott, Phil. *Hemingway's Hurricane: The Great Florida Keys Storm of 1935*. Camden, ME: International Marine, 2006.

Sheeran, Chris and Leonard Paul. "From 1939: 20 known dead in train wreck." *Elko Daily Free Press*, 13 August 1939. Reprint. Available at https://www.rgj .com/story/life/2014/07/08/known-dead-train-wreck/12318557/. Accessed 26 January 2019.

Sjostrom, Jan. "A Titanic Legacy: Exhibit Explores Life of Henry Flagler." *Palm Beach Daily News*, 18 November 2013. Available at https://www.palmbeach dailynews.com/news/national/titanic-legacy-exhibit-explores-life-henry -flagler/G1FwrndHapBr204YujOlDJ/. Accessed 25 August 2018.

Southern Pacific Company. *Our Dining Car Recipes*. San Francisco: Southern Pacific Company, 1930.

Southern Pacific Passenger Trains: The "City of San Francisco." Available at http:// espee.railfan.net/cosf.html. Accessed 21 January 2019.

Standiford, Les. *Last Train to Paradise: Henry Flagler and the Spectacular Rise and Fall of the Railroad That Crossed an Ocean*. New York: Broadway Books, 2003.

———. *Water to the Angels: William, His Monumental Aqueduct, and the Rise of Los Angeles*. New York: Ecco Press. Reprint, 2016.

Stringfellow, Kim. *Greetings from the Salton Sea: Folly and Intervention in the Southern California Landscape, 1905–2005*. Staunton, VA: Center for American Places—Center Books on the American West, 2011. Available at http://greetingsfromsaltonsea.com/. Accessed 30 September 2019.

"Tacoma Narrows Bridge Collapse 'Gallopin' Gertie.'" YouTube (website). Available at https://www.youtube.com/watch?v=j-zczJXSxnw. Accessed 9 October 2019.

von Hardenberg, Wilko Graf. "Expecting Disaster: The 1963 Landslide of the Vajont Dam." In Environment & Society Portal, *Arcadia* (2011), no. 8. Munich, Ger.: Rachel Carson Center for Environment and Society. Available at http://www.environmentandsociety.org/arcadia/expecting-disaster -1963-landslide-vajont-dam. Accessed 10 October 2019.

Walker, Sally M. *Sinking the* Sultana. Somerville, MA: Candlewick Press, 2017.

Washington State Department of Transportation. "Tacoma Narrows Bridge: Eyewitness Accounts." Available at https://www.wsdot.wa.gov/TNBhistory /People/eyewitness.htm. Accessed 10 October 2019.

Wayner, Robert J. *Car Names, Numbers and Consists*. New York: Wayner Publica- tions, 1972.

Wilkman, Jon. *Floodpath: The Deadliest Man-Made Disaster of 20th-Century American and the Making of Modern Los Angeles*. New York: Bloomsbury, 2016.

IMAGE CREDITS

CHAPTER 1

Andersonville Prison survivor (p. 2). Public domain. Available at https://upload
.wikimedia.org/wikipedia/commons/5/5a/Andersonvillesurvivor.jpg.

Steamship *Sultana* at Memphis, April 26, 1865 (p. 3). Credited to Thomas W.
Bankes, Helena, AR. Public domain. Available at https://commons.wikimedia
.org/wiki/File:Civil_War_Steamer_Sultana_tintype,_1865.png.

The *Sultana* on fire (p. 10). Illustration from *Harper's Weekly*, May 20, 1865,
316. Public domain. Available at https://commons.wikimedia.org/wiki
/File:Explosion_of_the_steamer_SULTANA,_April_28,_1865_LCCN2002
699583.jpg.

Schematic of a cylindrical water boiler (p. 17). HMSO – January 1901, October
1907, this edition April 1912. *Stokers' Manual*, 1912, Admiralty via HMSO,
via Eyre & Spottiswoode. This work created by the United Kingdom
Government is in the public domain. Available at https://en.wikipedia.org/wiki
/Scotch_marine_boiler#/media/File:Scotch_marine_boiler_side_section
_(Stokers_Manual_1912).jpg.

CHAPTER 2

Newly completed Tay Bridge (p. 21). Public domain. National Library of Scotland.
Available at https://commons.wikimedia.org/wiki/File:Tay_Bridge_from
north(5180825545).jpg.

Aftermath of the bridge collapse (p. 30). Public domain. National Library of
Scotland. Available at https://commons.wikimedia.org/wiki/Category:Tay
_Bridge_disaster#/media/File:Fallen_girders,_Tay_Bridge.jpg.

Illustration of the rescue and recovery efforts (p. 32). Public domain. Available at https://commons.wikimedia.org/wiki/File:Catastrophe_du_pont_sur_le _Tay_-_1879_-_Illustration.jpg.

Recovered locomotive no. 224 (p. 33). Public domain. Dundee Central Library. Available at https://en.wikipedia.org/wiki/File:North_British_Railway _locomotive_224.jpg.

Ruins of the Tay Bridge (p. 36). Public domain. Available at https://commons .wikimedia.org/wiki/File:Fallen_girders,_Tay_Bridge_(5180825769).jpg.

CHAPTER 3

Map of the All-American Canal (p. 44). Public domain. Available at https://commons .wikimedia.org/wiki/File:All_american_canal_map.png.

Contemporary map of the Imperial Valley by Clarence Everett Tait (p. 48). Public domain. Available at https://commons.wikimedia.org/w/index.php?curid =14496928.

Diagram of the "Mexican Cut" (p. 50). Public domain. Available at https://commons .wikimedia.org/w/index.php?curid=14496928.

Photograph of the flooding and waterfall created by the Mexican Cut (p. 53). Public domain, courtesy of Imperial Irrigation District.

Southern Pacific railway cars (p. 54). Public domain, courtesy of Imperial Irrigation District.

The new river flooding the Imperial Valley, 1907 (p. 55). Public domain, courtesy of Imperial Irrigation District.

A modern view of the All-American Canal (p. 59). Public domain. Photo by Charles O'Rear, US National Archives. Available at https://commons.wikimedia .org/w/index.php?curid=17089422.

Modern desilting works along the All-American Canal (p. 60). Public domain. Photo by Andy Pernick, US Bureau of Reclamation. Available at https://creative commons.org/licenses/by-sa/2.0.

CHAPTER 4

Façade of the Mulholland Dam (p. 62). Public domain. Library of Congress. Available at https://commons.wikimedia.org/wiki/File:BEAR _ORNAMENTS_ON_DOWNSTREAM_SIDE_OF_DAM_-_Los _Angeles_Aqueduct,_Mulholland_Dam,_Los_Angeles,_Los_Angeles _County,_CA_HAER_CA-298-AL-3.tif.

William Mulholland with tripod (p. 63). Public domain. Photo by James Bledsoe. Courtesy USC Library. Available at http://digitallibrary.usc.edu/cdm/singleitem /collection/p15799coll65/id/3543.

St. Francis Dam at full pool (p. 66). Public domain. Photo by H. T. Stearns. Available at https://commons.wikimedia.org/w/index.php?curid=10829037.

Destroyed railway in Castaic Junction (p. 74). Public domain. USGS. Available at https://www.flickr.com/photos/usgeologicalsurvey/11449413284/.

Photo of "The Tombstone" (p. 80). Public domain. Available at https://commons .wikimedia.org/wiki/File:Standing_section.jpg.

Photo of Hollywood Reservoir and Mulholland Dam (p. 82). Public domain.

Photo by Clinton Steeds. Available at https://commons.wikimedia.org/w /index.php?curid=6930927.

CHAPTER 5

Portrait of Henry Flagler (p. 90). Public domain. *The Cyclopedia of American Biography*, vol. 8 (New York: The Press Association Compilers, 1918), 22. Available at https://archive.org/stream/cyclopaediaofame08wilsuoft#page /n55/mode/2up.

Hotel Ponce de Leon (now Flagler College). (P. 95.) Public domain. Available at https://commons.wikimedia.org/wiki/File:Flagler_College-Hotel_Ponce_de _Leon.JPG.

Royal Palm Hotel, Miami (p. 97). Public domain. *A Guide to Florida for Tourists, Sportsmen, and Settlers* (1912), 240. Available at https://commons.wikimedia .org/wiki/File:Royal_Palm_Hotel,_Miami_(1912).jpg.

Laborers on Key West railway extension (p. 101). Public domain. Available at http://fpc.dos.state.fl.us/reference/rc14050.jpg.

Long Key Viaduct (p. 103). Public domain. Key West News Company/State Archives of Florida/Florida Memory. Released to the public domain in the United States under the terms of 257.35(6) Florida Statutes. Available at https//www.floridamemory.com/items/show/159331.

Henry Flagler arriving in Key West (p. 104). Public domain. Courtesy Florida Keys Public Libraries.

Illustration of the Over-Sea Railway during the Labor Day Hurricane (p. 111). Public domain. In Russian Empire magazine *Nature and People*, no. 29 & 30 (1915).

Destruction along the railway (p. 113). Public domain. Key West News Company/State Archives of Florida/Florida Memory. Released to the public domain in the United States under the terms of 257.35(6) Florida Statutes. Available at https://www.floridamemory.com/items/show/149572.

CHAPTER 6

"City of San Francisco" poster (p. 122). Public domain. Available at https://commons .wikimedia.org/wiki/File:City_of_San_Francisco_SP_Advertisement_1938.jpg.

Daylight lounge car photo (p. 124). Public domain. Available at https://commons .wikimedia.org/wiki/File:Daylight_lounge_car.jpg.

"City of San Francisco" in Oakland, CA, station (p. 127). Public domain. From Erle Heath, *Seventy-Five Years of Progress: Historical Sketch of the Southern Pacific* (San Francisco: Southern Pacific Railroad, 1938), 39.

The wreck of the "City of San Francisco" (p. 130). Public domain. Courtesy Nevada Historical Society.

CHAPTER 7

Tacoma Narrows Bridge (p. 143). Public domain. Courtesy Washington State Historical Society.

Steel tie-down cables anchoring the bridge (p. 144). Public domain. Available at http://www.tacomanarrowsbridge.org/photos1940.html.

Man running from bridge collapse (p. 151). Public domain. Courtesy University of Washington Libraries, Special Collections, University Archives Division. PH Coll. 290.39b.

The moment of the bridge collapse (p. 152). Public domain. Courtesy University of Washington Libraries, Special Collections, University Archives Division. PH Coll. 290.36.

Aftermath of the bridge collapse (p. 154). Public domain. Courtesy Washington State Archives.

Broken strands of main cable (p. 155). Public domain. Courtesy Washington State Archives.

Modern new Tacoma Narrows Bridges (p. 160). Public domain. Photo by Jessica Spengler. Available at https://commons.wikimedia.org/wiki/File:Tacoma_Narrows_Bridge,_Seattle_to_Portland_by_train2.jpg.

CHAPTER 8

Modern view of Vajont Dam (p. 162). Public domain. Available at https://commons.wikimedia.org/wiki/File:Diga_del_Vajont_.jpg.

Aftermath of the landslide (p. 168). Public domain. Available at https://commons.wikimedia.org/wiki/File:Vajont_frana_.jpg.

View of the Vajont Dam from the valley below (p. 173). Public domain. Foto di Emanuele Paolini. Available at https://commons.wikimedia.org/wiki/File:La_diga_del_Vajont_vista_da_Longarone_18-8-2005.jpg.

INDEX